D1565525

Schumpeter and the Endogeneity of Technology

Joseph Schumpeter was, beyond doubt, one of the most creative and influential economists of the twentieth century. That influence has increased significantly since his death in 1950. Schumpeter directly addressed the central question of how some societies have managed to achieve substantial improvements in material wellbeing. His answer to this question, with its emphasis on conditions favoring innovation, has become even more persuasive given the course of world history post-1945.

Nathan Rosenberg argues that today Schumpeter speaks to economists in an even more authoritative way for yet another reason.

This book explores Schumpeter's views as an economist who was, long ago, committed to the notion of the endogeneity of technology. His mature writings offer illuminating historical analyses of how and why some social systems have managed to generate innovation. This element of his vision deserves far more attention than it has so far received, and this book redresses the balance. Moreover, bringing us up-to-date, Nathan Rosenberg explores the ways in which the concept of endogeneity illuminates recent American economic history.

Nathan Rosenberg is Professor of Economics at Stanford University. His publications include *How the West Grew Rich* (with L. E. Birdzell, Jr.), *Inside the Black Box, Exploring the Black Box*, and, most recently, *Paths of Innovation* (with David Mowery). He is the recipient of honorary degrees from the universities of Lund and Bologna, and he was awarded the Leonardo da Vinci Prize for his contributions to the history of technology. He is past chairman of the Stanford Economics Department, a fellow of the Canadian Institute for Advanced Research, and a member of the board of directors and the executive board of the National Bureau of Economic Research.

The Graz Schumpeter Lectures

1 Evolutionary Economics and Creative Destruction
J. Stanley Metcalfe

2 Knowledge, Institutions and Evolution in Economics
Brian J. Loesby

3 Schumpeter and the Endogeneity of Technology
Some American Perspectives
Nathan Rosenberg

Schumpeter and the Endogeneity of Technology

Some American perspectives

Nathan Rosenberg

London and New York

First published
2000 by Routledge
11 New Fetter Lane, London EC4P 4EE

Simultaneously published in the USA and Canada
by Routledge
29 West 35th Street, New York, NY 10001

Routledge is an imprint of the Taylor & Francis Group

© 2000 Nathan Rosenberg

Typeset in Sabon by The Running Head Limited,
www.therunninghead.com
Printed and bound in Great Britain by
TJ International Ltd, Padstow, Cornwall

British Library Cataloguing in Publication Data
A catalogue record for this book is available from the British Library

Library of Congress Cataloging-in-Publication Data
Rosenberg, Nathan, 1927–
  Schumpeter and the endogeneity of technology : some American
  perspectives / Nathan Rosenberg.
  (Graz Schumpeter lectures ; 3)
  Includes bibliographical references and index.
  1. Schumpeter, Joseph Alois, 1883–1950. 2. Evolutionary economics.
  3. Institutional economics. 4. Technological innovations–Economic
  aspects–United States. I. Title. II. Series.
  HB101.S3 R67 2000
  338′.064 21–dc21   99–046088

ISBN 0–415–22652–X

Contents

Tables

Acknowledgments

It was a great pleasure to have had the opportunity to deliver the Graz Schumpeter lectures in a city, and at a university, where Schumpeter had himself once spent a great deal of his time. I am most grateful for the intellectual hospitality as well as the personal warmth that were extended to me and to my wife, Rina, during my stay at the University of Graz. I wish to thank Professor Heinz D. Kurz, Chairman of the Graz Schumpeter Society, and the members of the Economics Department for making my visit such a thoroughly enjoyable one.

In preparing this volume I have been the fortunate beneficiary of numerous discussions with my distinguished colleague Moses Abramovitz. Stanley Engerman read and offered valuable comments on an earlier draft of the book. On a number of more specific matters I am pleased to acknowledge the assistance of Timothy Bresnahan, Kenneth Arrow, Zvi Griliches, Manuel Trajtenberg, David Mowery, Scott Stern, Christophe Lecuyer, Karl Habermeier, Ashish Arora, Alfonso Gambardella, Ralph Landau, Richard Nelson, and George Akerlof.

The Canadian Institute for Advanced Research provided generous financial support that was essential to the completion of this book. Chapter 5 is a shortened version of a paper that originally appeared in *General Purpose Technologies and Economic Growth*, edited by Elhanan Helpman and published by MIT Press in 1998.

Chapter 1

Joseph Schumpeter and the economic interpretation of history

Introduction

It is common to say of Schumpeter that he was a lover of paradox. Indeed, that statement has been made by no less an authority on Schumpeter than Schumpeter himself. In his preface to the first edition of *Capitalism, Socialism and Democracy*, he informs his reader that Part II of his book will deal with the "inevitable decomposition of capitalist society." But he adds that, contrary to the views of Marx and others, his own analysis will lead the reader to the author's "paradoxical conclusion: capitalism is being killed by its achievements."[1]

I do not intend, in this chapter, to evaluate the validity of that conclusion, even with the "easy" wisdom of a retrospective view of more than fifty years. I do, however, want to take this opportunity to examine Schumpeter's views on the analysis of economic change, the forces that give rise to such change, and to the power of economic changes to generate other changes in the context of advanced capitalist societies.

I should emphasize that most of my attention to Schumpeter will be focused on his later writings (Schumpeter died in January 1950). Schumpeter's views on a number of economic issues changed substantially over the course of his lifetime. Indeed, it would be astonishing if this were not the case, since Schumpeter's adult years covered the whole of the first half of the twentieth century, during which time, to put it mildly, many things changed. Not the least of these is that, when Schumpeter published *Capitalism, Socialism and Democracy* in 1942, the Habsburgs and the Austro-Hungarian Empire were long since gone, and the economic universe looked very different from the vantage point of Cambridge, Massachusetts in

1940 than it did from Vienna, Bonn or Graz in 1910 or 1920. Indeed, it not only looked very different; it was very different.

To cite one very important change in perspective, the younger Schumpeter, and even the Schumpeter who wrote the massive, two-volume work on *Business Cycles* in the 1930s, went to great pains to distinguish between innovation and invention, and to insist that he had no analytical interest in the determinants of inventive activity. He saw invention as exogenous. But when he wrote *Capitalism, Socialism and Democracy*, he expressed a very different view, and forcefully argued that the modern corporation had, in effect, endogenized inventive activity. This issue is one to which I shall return in my second chapter.

It is obvious that Schumpeter's writings have not been neglected since his death. Indeed, I am confident that a citation analysis of the economic literature would show that Schumpeter is receiving far more attention today than he did in the last decade or so of his life. Perhaps, as a long-time admirer, I should not look this particular gift-horse (i.e., the gift-horse of Schumpeter's posthumous popularity) in the mouth. Nevertheless, it is my intention to do so, partly – but only partly – because the overwhelming bulk of the literature on the "Schumpeterian hypothesis," written by people who are sometimes called "neo-Schumpeterians," deals with only a very small portion of Schumpeter's writings, and neglects much else that is of great value.

One of Schumpeter's most enduring intellectual strengths is that he looked at economic activity from a larger frame of reference. This frame encompassed not only a sophisticated sociology of capitalist life and institutions (heavily influenced, I would note, by his central European origins) but was also specifically historical in nature. Indeed, I am tempted to argue that Schumpeter's historical perspective constituted one of his greatest strengths as an economist. Once again my authority for this statement is Schumpeter himself. Early in his monumental *History of Economic Analysis*, Schumpeter observed that a "scientific" economist is to be identified by the demonstrated command over three fields – history, statistics, and theory. He then went on to say:

> Of these fundamental fields, economic history – which issues into and includes present-day facts – is by far the most important. I wish to state right now that if, starting my work in economics afresh, I were told that I could study only one of the three but

have my choice, it would be economic history that I should choose. And this on three grounds. First, the subject matter of economics is essentially a unique process in historic time. Nobody can hope to understand the economic phenomena of any, including the present, epoch who has not an adequate command of historical facts and an adequate amount of historical sense or of what may be described as historical experience. Second, the historical report cannot be purely economic; therefore it affords the best method for understanding how economic and non-economic facts are related to one another and how the various social sciences should be related to one another. Third, it is, I believe, the fact that most of the fundamental errors currently committed in economic analysis are due to a lack of historical experience more often than to any other shortcoming of the economist's equipment.[2]

I must observe sadly that, today, not even a minimal knowledge of history is regarded as essential to the training of professional economists at most American universities, although I am pleased to say that my own university, Stanford, still retains a history requirement for its graduate students in economics. Clearly, Schumpeter still has much to teach us, not just about the uses of economics to history, but about the uses of history to economics.

It should, I believe, be obvious that the author of a distinguished two-volume work on the history of business cycles had the qualifications to be called an economic historian. However, I wish to stake a much stronger claim with respect to the entire corpus of Schumpeter's work: in his view, the very subject matter of economics is history. Economics is about economic change as it has occurred over historical time. That is why he insists upon the importance of studying capitalism as an evolutionary process. It is also why he assigns such a limited importance to the study of stationary economic processes. (Parenthetically, I must admit that here Schumpeter presents yet another paradox: simultaneously holding the view that economics is about economic change while also ranking Walras as the greatest of all economists. I will say more about this later.) And Schumpeter's view, that the subject matter of economics is history, has a great deal to do with his very high regard for some of Marx's contributions to economic analysis. You will remember that the four chapters that make up Part I of *Capitalism, Socialism and Democracy* are devoted entirely to an examination of Marx's work.

I believe that the best explanation of Schumpeter's frequent expressions of admiration for and intellectual indebtedness to Marx is contained in the following statement:

> There is . . . one thing of fundamental importance for the methodology of economics which he actually achieved. Economists always have either themselves done work in economic history or else used the historical work of others. But the facts of economic history were assigned to a separate compartment. They entered theory, if at all, merely in the role of illustrations, or possibly of verification of results. They mixed with it only mechanically. Now Marx's mixture is a chemical one; that is to say, he introduced them into the very argument that produces the results. He was the first economist of top rank to see and to teach systematically how economic theory may be turned into historical analysis and how the historical narrative may be turned into *histoire raisonée.*"[3]

Invaluable working hypotheses

Now, although Schumpeter was indeed an admirer of Marx, he was also always careful to distinguish between the writings of Marx and what he liked to call "vulgar Marxism." He defended Marx against some of the less-informed criticisms of the economic interpretation, such as the crudely reductionist view that it reduces all human behavior to narrowly-based economic motives, or that economic materialism was somehow logically incompatible with metaphysical or religious beliefs. With that distinction in mind, I want to suggest that Schumpeter, like Marx, believed in the economic interpretation of history. Indeed, I want to suggest that Schumpeter developed what an econometrician might call a "reduced form" of the economic interpretation, which amounted to two propositions, and in so doing eliminated the centrality of class warfare that dominated Marx's own writings:

1   "The forms or conditions of production are the fundamental determinant of social structures which in turn breed attitudes, actions and civilization."
2   "The forms of production themselves have a logic of their own; that is to say, they change according to necessities inherent in them so as to produce their successors merely by their own

working."⁴ Much earlier, in his *Theory of Economic Development*, Schumpeter had stated that "the economic world is relatively autonomous because it takes up such a great part of a nation's life, and forms or conditions a great part of the remainder."⁵

Schumpeter asserted that "Both propositions undoubtedly contain a large amount of truth and are, as we shall find at several turns of our way, invaluable working hypotheses."⁶ His main "qualification," if indeed one wishes to call it a qualification, is his insistence upon the importance of lags, i.e., social forms that persist long after they have lost their original economic rationale. It is far from clear that Marx would have disagreed with such a qualification, since Marx was, in my view, much too sophisticated a historian to believe that economic changes generated the "appropriate" social changes instantaneously. Indeed, in making the qualification about lags, Schumpeter himself absolves Marx of such possible naiveté, adding that Marx, although perhaps not fully appreciating the significance of lags, would not have taken the simplistic position involved in denying them a role.

> Social structures, types and attitudes are coins that do not readily melt. Once they are formed they persist, possibly for centuries, and since structures and types display different degrees of this ability to survive, we almost always find that actual group and national behavior more or less departs from what we should expect it to be if we tried to infer it from the dominant forms of the productive process. Though this applies quite generally, it is most clearly seen when a highly durable structure transfers itself bodily from one country to another. The social situation created in Sicily by the Norman conquest will illustrate my meaning. Such facts Marx did not overlook but he hardly realized all their implications.⁷

The capstone of Schumpeter's own articulation of the economic interpretation of history appears in the closing paragraph of Chapter 11 of *Capitalism, Socialism and Democracy*, "The Civilization of Capitalism." In that paragraph Schumpeter declares:

> However, whether favorable or unfavorable, value judgments about capitalist performance are of little interest. For mankind

is not free to choose. . . . Things economic and social move
by their own momentum and the ensuing situations compel
individuals and groups to behave in certain ways whatever they
may wish to do – not indeed by destroying their freedom of
choice but by shaping the choosing mentalities and by narrow-
ing the list of possibilities from which to choose. If this is
the quintessence of Marxism then we all of us have got to be
Marxists.[8]

In these chapters I will argue that we all of us do indeed have to
be Marxists, at least in Schumpeter's carefully restricted sense in
the paragraph just quoted. In subsequent chapters I will attempt to
demonstrate the enduring value of this Schumpeterian perspective.
And also, as it should hardly be necessary to add, this restricted form
of Marxism has nothing to do with the centrally directed economies of eastern Europe, whose collapse we have recently had such
good cause to celebrate. The two propositions of Schumpeter's
economic interpretation of history need to be regarded as nothing
more nor less than what Schumpeter said they were, i.e., they are
"invaluable working hypotheses."

If it is correct, as I have asserted, that Schumpeter shared a
"stripped down" version of Marx's economic interpretation of
history, it must also be true that Schumpeter shared with Marx a
common vision of capitalism as a social system that possessed its
own internal logic, and that, consequently, also underwent a process
of self-transformation. Indeed, it is precisely this internal logic that
renders the economic interpretation such an invaluable working
hypothesis. This self-transformation resulted from certain "laws of
motion," as Marx called them, which were inherent in capitalism as
a social system. Thus, it was possible to understand the dynamics
of capitalism as the system actually behaved over the course of
historical time if one could only grasp these laws of motion. In
other words, Schumpeter believed that it was possible to develop
an economic theory that would account for the broad contours
of economic change. This stood, of course, in stark contrast to the
static equilibrium model prevailing in academic economics during
Schumpeter's own mature years, a model that examined how the
economy re-established itself, rather mechanically, to its equilibrium
position after being displaced by some small disturbance.

This is an appropriate place to make a rather dogmatic statement – dogmatic because I do not have the time to marshal fully

the evidence in support of the statement: Schumpeter's analysis of innovation is fundamentally a disequilibrium analysis, which continually (or, more precisely, intermittently) bursts out of the confines of static equilibrium analysis. Consequently, in Schumpeter's view, economic analyses that remain within that restrictive framework can provide only modest insights into the innovation process. Schumpeter had already stated in 1911 that:

> "static" analysis is not only unable to predict the consequences of discontinuous changes in the traditional ways of doing things; it can neither explain the occurrence of such productive revolutions nor the phenomena which accompany them. It can only investigate the new equilibrium position after the changes have occurred.[9]

As a closely related point, I would like to assert that much of the literature on the "Schumpeterian hypothesis" involves a misreading of Part II of *Capitalism, Socialism and Democracy*. Schumpeter was not arguing that monopoly is the most congenial market environment for innovation. His argument, rather, was that innovation commonly creates monopoly, but these monopolies are only temporary – mere epiphenomena thrown up by the inherent technological dynamism of advanced capitalist economies. Schumpeter's deeper point, so brilliantly sketched out in Chapter 7 ("The Process of Creative Destruction") is the inability of static equilibrium analysis to capture the essential long-term features of capitalist reality.

Schumpeter spoke revealingly of his grand intellectual aims in addressing the audience of the Japanese translation of his *Theory of Economic Development* (1937). He observed in the preface to that edition:

> If my Japanese readers asked me before opening the book what it is that I was aiming at when I wrote it, more than a quarter of a century ago, I would answer that I was trying to construct a theoretic model of the process of economic change in time, or perhaps more clearly, to answer the question how the economic system generates the force which incessantly transforms it . . . I felt very strongly . . . that there was a source of energy within the economic system which would of itself disrupt any equilibrium that might be attained. If this is so, then there must be a purely economic theory of economic change which does

not merely rely on external factors propelling the economic system from one equilibrium to another.[10]

This statement of intellectual purpose would also have served as an apt prolegomenon to Marx's work. Indeed, there are some striking parallels in Marx's preface to the original German edition of *Capital*. But Schumpeter himself, in the paragraph immediately following the one from which I have just quoted, calls attention to the similarities. Speaking of his own vision of a "purely economic theory of economic change," he goes on to say that

> this idea and this aim are exactly the same as the idea and the aim which underlie the economic teaching of Karl Marx. In fact, what distinguishes him from the economists of his own time and those who preceded him, was precisely a vision of economic evolution as a distinct process generated by the economic system itself.[11]

Of course, one can go further in pointing to several of Marx's primary concerns that were also primary concerns of Schumpeter's analysis of economic change under capitalism:

1   the inevitability of growth in the size of the firm and in industrial concentration, a central theme of *Capitalism, Socialism and Democracy*;
2   the inherent instability of capitalism and the inevitability of "crises," Schumpeter's major concern, as embodied in his most ambitious work, *Business Cycles*;
3   the eventual destruction of capitalist institutions, and the arrival of a socialist form of economic organization, as a result of the working out of the internal logic of capitalist evolution, a theme intimately connected with the growth of industrial bigness, spelled out in detail in *Capitalism, Socialism and Democracy*.

I am anxious, however, not to ruin what I regard as a good argument by overstatement. You are of course familiar with fundamental differences between these two seminal figures. The "details" of the process of economic change that are visualized by Marx as leading to socialism, involve the increasing misery of the proletariat; whereas, for Schumpeter, it is precisely the highly successful economic performance of capitalism that, again paradoxically, generates political and social forces leading to "crumbling walls" (the title of Chapter 12 of *Capitalism, Socialism and Democracy*) and eventual breakdown. At the same time, Schumpeter himself was anxious to point out that, in certain respects at least, it is easy to exaggerate the differences between his own analysis and that of Marx:

> The capitalist process not only destroys its own institutional framework but it also creates the conditions for another. Destruction may not be the right word after all. Perhaps I should have spoken of transformation. The outcome of the process is not simply a void that could be filled by whatever might happen to turn up; things and souls are transformed in such a way as to become increasingly amenable to the socialist form of life. With every peg from under the capitalist structure vanishes an impossibility of the socialist plan. In both these respects Marx's vision was right ... In the end there is not so much difference as one might think between saying that the decay of capitalism is due to its success and saying that it is due to its failure.[12]

Again, a nice paradoxical formulation.

The endogeneity of innovation

I now propose to examine certain elements of Schumpeter's theory of economic change against the specific backdrop of his economic interpretation of history. First, capitalism has to be understood as an evolutionary system rather than as a system that continually reverts to some equilibrium after small departures from it. More specifically, this evolution is a reflection of certain dynamic forces that Schumpeter, along with Marx, believes are inherent in the incentive structure, the pursuit of profits, and the competitive institutions that lie at the basis of capitalism. The implications of this view, not least for economic theory, are profound, because any system of analysis that abstracts from the forces generating economic change is also abstracting from the very essence of the economic system that is called capitalism. On this point Schumpeter is anxious to associate himself with Marx and to remind his readers that the theories of perfect and imperfect competition, that were being polished in the two Cambridges during the 1930s and after, were guilty of totally neglecting the central feature of capitalism.

> Capitalism . . . is by nature a form or method of economic change and not only never is but never can be stationary. And this evolutionary character of the capitalist process is not merely due to the fact that economic life goes on in a social and natural environment which changes and by its change alters the data of economic action; this fact is important and these changes (wars, revolutions and so on) often condition industrial change, but they are not its prime movers. Nor is this evolutionary character due to a quasi-automatic increase in population and capital or to the vagaries of monetary systems of which exactly the same thing holds true.[13]

Schumpeter's criticisms of the theories of perfect competition, imperfect competition, and monopolistic competition flow directly from this view of capitalism. Of the conclusion, drawn from the theory of imperfect competition, that the typical firm will be sub-optimally small, Schumpeter sardonically observes: "Since imperfect competition is . . . held to be an outstanding characteristic of modern industry we are set to wondering what world these theorists live in, unless fringe-end cases are all they have in mind."[14]

The implications of this view are, for Schumpeter, very far-reaching. For, as he goes on to argue, it renders essentially irrelevant that view of the competitive process that concerns itself with "how capitalism administers existing structures" since "the relevant problem is how it creates and destroys them." As soon as this is recognized, one's "outlook on capitalist practice and its social results changes considerably." In particular, it is essential to understand that the competition that really matters is not price competition among a large number of firms producing a homogeneous product. Rather, it is

> the competition from the new commodity, the new technology, the new source of supply, the new type of organization (the largest-scale unit of control for instance) – competition which commands a decisive cost or quality advantage and which strikes not at the margins of the profits and the outputs of the existing firms but at their foundations and their very lives.[15]

Thus, the main agency making for economic change is innovation, a phenomenon that is defined much more broadly, as the last quotation makes clear, than only technological innovation. Nevertheless, technological innovation is central to long-term economic change for Schumpeter, just as it had been for Marx. Moreover, Schumpeter and Marx share a common view on the determinants of science and technology that sets them distinctly apart from the main line of thinking in economics, where these have been treated as exogenous variables. Specifically, they regard the remarkable performances of both science and technology in the western world as having been overwhelmingly due to the incentive mechanisms of capitalism and the associated bourgeois culture. This is a subject to which I will return in a later chapter.

Schumpeter asserts in his later work that progress in both science and technology must be understood to have been endogenous to capitalism, as befits an economic interpretation of history, and he is at pains once again to associate this view with that of Marx. In an appreciative essay that he wrote in the *Journal of Political Economy* to commemorate the centenary of "The Communist Manifesto," he points out that Marx had "launched out on a panegyric upon bourgeois achievement that has no equal in economic literature." After quoting a relevant portion of the Marxist text, he says:

> No reputable "bourgeois" economist of that or any other time – certainly not A. Smith or J. S. Mill – ever said as much as this. Observe, in particular, the emphasis upon the creative role of the business class that the majority of the most "bourgeois" economists so persistently overlooked and of the business class as such, whereas most of us would, on the one hand, also insert into the picture non-bourgeois contributions to the bourgeois success – the contributions of non-bourgeois bureaucracies, for instance – and, on the other hand, commit the mistake (for such I believe it is) to list as *independent* factors science and technology, whereas Marx's sociology enabled him to see that these as well as "progress" in such fields as education and hygiene were just as much the products of the bourgeois class culture – hence, ultimately, of the business class – as was the business performance itself.[16]

In Schumpeter's view, the rationalizing influence of the capitalistic mentality and institutions created "the growth of rational science" as well as its "long list of applications."[17] Significantly, Schumpeter cites as examples not only "airplanes, refrigerators, television and that sort of thing" but also the "modern hospital." Although one might be surprised at the appearance here of an institution that was not, at least in the past, ordinarily operated on a profit-making basis, Schumpeter's explanation is illuminating and certainly provocative.

[It is] fundamentally because capitalist rationality supplied the habits of mind that evolved the methods used in these hospitals. And the victories, not yet completely won but in the offing, over cancer, syphilis and tuberculosis will be as much capitalist achievements as motorcars or pipe lines or Bessemer steel have been. In the case of medicine, there is a capitalist profession behind the methods, capitalist both because to a large extent it works in a business spirit and because it is an emulsion of the industrial and commercial bourgeoisie. But even if that were not so, modern medicine and hygiene would still be by-products of the capitalist process just as is modern education.[18]

Thus, Schumpeter's Weltanschauung is one in which science and technology, normally so far from the world of phenomena examined by the neo-classical economics of his own time, are in reality highly endogenous to the capitalist world. This is so because they have become subject not only to the gravitational pull of economic forces, but also to the "habits of mind" inculcated by the rationalizing forces of the capitalist market place.

But Schumpeter went much farther down the road of the economic interpretation than any major twentieth-century economist and, in some respects, perhaps even farther than Marx. He seems to have been driven in this direction by his determination to state the strongest possible case for the dominating role of the innovative process in the generation of economic growth. I am thinking in particular here of the determinants of consumer preferences. Although Marx of course heaped the viles of his bilious wrath upon "commodity fetishism" under capitalism, Schumpeter was prepared to argue, quite forcefully, not only that tastes as well as technology were endogenous, and the consequence of entrepreneurial initiatives, but also that economists had a professional obligation to study the determinants of changing consumers' choices.

Innovations in the economic system do not as a rule take place in such a way that first new wants arise spontaneously in consumers and then the productive apparatus swings round through their pressure. We do not deny the presence of this nexus. It is, however, the producer who as a rule initiates economic change, and consumers are educated by him if necessary; they are, as it were, taught to want new things, or things which differ in some respect or other from those which they have been in the habit of using. Therefore, while it is permissible and even necessary to consider consumers' wants as an independent and indeed the fundamental force in a theory of the circular flow, we must take a different attitude as soon as we analyse change.[19]

I must confess that I do not find this argument persuasive. It is a specimen of the sort of reasoning that I had in mind earlier, when I spoke of the hazard of ruining a good argument by overstatement. Surely the pool of people, and firms, with inventive capabilities are strongly influenced, in deciding in which categories to direct their inventive talent, by the size of the prospective market in particular product categories. And, equally surely, the mere rise in incomes in the course of economic growth will disclose some product categories with higher income elasticities of demand, and therefore potentially larger, more rapidly growing markets, than others.

Schumpeter makes the observation elsewhere that "railroads have not emerged because any consumers took the initiative in displaying an effective demand for their service in preference to the services of mail coaches."[20] This is no more than a caricature. Of course consumers did not demand a specific form of improved transportation to replace the inefficient services of mail coaches. But gradually rising incomes powerfully focused inventive activity on the category of faster modes of transportation; and the growth of an increasingly affluent population in a richly endowed country of continental proportions, where high transportation costs were a serious impediment to improved economic efficiency, had a great deal to do with American leadership in the exploitation of a succession of transportation improvements. This was true regardless of where the improvements originated – steamboats, railroads, automobiles, airplanes. This is a subject that was examined with great insight some years ago by Jacob Schmookler.[21]

Whatever our scepticism, however, it is worth noting that Schumpeter's views concerning the shaping of consumer tastes serve to reinforce his commitment to an economic interpretation of historical change. Thus, if tastes do not stand as independently determined, but as malleable social phenomena that are shaped by economic forces, they need to be regarded as part of the research agenda of economists. This is, of course, a position that would be emphatically rejected by most neo-classical economists. Their view is simply that the market behavior of consumers can be adequately accounted for by reference to observable economic variables such as changes in prices and income, a view that was forcefully formulated some years ago by Stigler and Becker.[22]

It should be added that, given the "malleability of tastes," as Schumpeter saw it, freedom of consumer choice is really a much overrated virtue. As he stated in 1949:

> Ever since the physiocrats (and before), economists have pro-fessed unbounded respect for the consumers' choice – is it not time to investigate what the bases for this respect are and how far the traditional and, in part, advertisement-shaped tastes of people are subject to the qualification that they might prefer other things than those which they want at present as soon as they have acquired familiarity with these other things? In matters of education, health, and housing there is almost practical un-animity about this – but might the principle not be carried much further?[23]

Filial piety?

Schumpeter's writings, and especially the centrality of his commit-ment to an economic interpretation of history and the implications that he drew from that interpretation, appeared to place him on a direct collision course with the main line of neo-classical thinking going back to Walras. If one accepts his view that "capitalist real-ity is first and last a process of change,"[24] then doesn't this leave stationary equilibrium analysis – the analysis of a world in which there are neither innovations nor entrepreneurs – in an irrelevant state? Schumpeter's response is as follows: "In appraising the per-formance of competitive enterprise, the question whether it would or would not tend to maximize production in a perfectly equilibrated stationary condition of the economic process is . . . almost, though not quite, irrelevant."[25]

The reason it is not completely irrelevant is that the model of a stationary competitive process is an invaluable guide to the behavior of a capitalist economy that possessed no internal forces generating economic change. Thus, the model of a Walrasian circular flow constitutes Schumpeter's starting-point in understanding the essential elements of capitalist reality precisely because it shows how the system would behave in the absence of its most distinctive feature – innovation. It is an indispensable abstraction because it makes it possible to trace out with greater precision the impact of innovative activity. The circular flow serves as the analytical starting-point for Schumpeter's theory of business cycles and growth, and the periodic tendency of the economic system to revert to an equilibrium is an essential part of that theory. But one cannot draw valid inferences from such an analysis about the efficiency with which actual capitalistic economies allocate resources. The analysis of a stationary economic process is justifiable as a starting-point for the study of capitalist markets and institutions, but not as a terminus. It explains how capitalist societies might behave if deprived of their central feature – innovation. Here one must keep prominently in mind Schumpeter's pithy observation: "Whereas a stationary feudal economy would still be a feudal economy, and a stationary socialist economy would still be a socialist economy, stationary capitalism is a contradiction in terms."[26]

All this can be read as a rather fundamental criticism of neoclassical economics. How then should one reconcile this with Schumpeter's numerous expressions of filial piety to Walras, and to his description of Walras' *Elements* as "this Magna Charta of exact economics"?[27] In his preface to the Japanese edition of the *Theory of Economic Development* Schumpeter stated of the Walrasian system: "I wish to emphasize that as an economist I owe more to it than to any other influence."[28] I have no completely satisfactory answer to the question posed. A flippant and unsatisfactory response would be to remind you once again that Schumpeter loved to be provocative in a deliberately paradoxical way. It is, after all, an equal paradox that Schumpeter, a man of deeply conservative instincts, should have written far more extensively, and far more convincingly, about the essential economic workability of a socialist society than did Marx, the foremost exponent of socialism.[29]

This is doubly ironic because, for reasons that Schumpeter of all people should have understood, centrally-directed socialist societies were economically unworkable. Moreover, a primary reason they were unworkable is that they could never learn how to exploit technological innovations.[30]

A more substantial response to the question of Schumpeter's devotion to Walras is the one that was already suggested. Schumpeter needed Walras' Magna Charta because its modeling of a strictly stationary economic process could be used to "floodlight" the impact of innovation. It was, in a sense, Schumpeter's Magna Charta for constructing his own model of the impact of innovation on the life of the economy. This is to be seen most clearly in Chapters II and III of his *Business Cycles*, where he goes to great (and rather tedious) lengths to demonstrate that, appropriately defined, a stationary state would be entirely free of forces generating cyclical behavior of any sort. The rigorous definition of that stationary state is what enables Schumpeter to draw the essential conclusion:

> Surely, nothing can be more plain or even more trite common sense than the proposition that innovation, as conceived by us, is at the center of practically all the phenomena, difficulties, and problems of economic life in capitalist society and that they, as well as the extreme sensitiveness of capitalism to disturbance, would be absent if productive resources flowed – either in unvarying or continuously increasing quantities – every year through substantially the same channels toward substantially the same goals, or were prevented from doing so only by external influences.[31]

A cynic might reply (and I confess here to a modicum of such cynicism) that Schumpeter needed to invoke Walras only to perform a sort of intellectual "deck-clearing" operation for his own intense focus upon an economic activity – innovation – that periodically disrupted the Walrasian circular flow. There is, clearly, more to it than that, even though it is worth remembering that deck-clearing can sometimes be a crucial intellectual activity. It was certainly more generally true that Schumpeter always held pure abstract theorizing in the highest esteem. There are, in fact, no fewer than 1,260 pages of evidence in support of this proposition in Schumpeter's monumental, posthumous book, *History of Economic Analysis*. Nevertheless, his great sensitivity to the limitations of neo-classical reasoning must have been intensified by his deep, early immersion in the works of the German Historical School.

In the German-speaking world of Schumpeter's formative years, the *Methodenstreit* between the historical and theoretical schools was a standing intellectual fact of life, and he was of course intimately familiar with, and respectful of, the works of Werner Sombart, Max Weber, and most particularly, Gustav Schmoller. In response to G. v. Below, a leading critic of the work of the historical school of German economists, Schumpeter commented: "it is certain that in all essentials Schmoller's work comes much nearer in displaying the true spirit of historical research and presents a much better grasp of its scope and use in economics."[32] Under these circumstances, Schumpeter might be expected to be well aware of the extreme limitations of an approach to economic life which made no serious pretense of dealing with economic behavior in real historical time. Thus, Schumpeter was in an excellent position to recognize the possibilities and the limitations of both the purely analytical and the purely historical approaches to economics.

This chapter has really been, in one respect, an attempt to call attention to the neglected dimensions of Schumpeter's views on historical change. Schumpeter was a scholar of great erudition, a scholar who had a profound grasp of several intellectual traditions. His own approach really involved a complex mixture of Marxism, Walrasian equilibrium analysis, and German historical scholarship. It was not a fusion of all three, because the three, in my opinion, are not capable of being completely fused. But it was a brilliant mixture, if not always an internally consistent one.

Chapter 2

Endogeneity in twentieth-century science and technology

Introduction

My purpose in this chapter is to suggest that both science and technology have been rendered a great deal more endogenous in the course of the twentieth century. I am not merely saying that science and technology have come to play roles of increasing importance in the economic life of advanced industrial economies, which is obvious. I am suggesting that this increasingly important role has been a direct consequence of institutional changes and associated changes in economic incentives. The manner in which new knowledge is transformed into goods and services of commercial value has become more directly connected to decision making processes on the part of maximizing agents responding to signals transmitted by normal market forces. I will develop my case primarily by drawing upon the American experience, but I would not want to be interpreted as suggesting that the American experience is necessarily representative of that of other industrial economies. The American experience, and the shaping of some of its dominant institutions, such as its universities, have differed in some significant ways from those of other industrial economies.

One can of course make the case that the general theme is not only a Schumpeterian theme but also a Marxian one. In his article in the *Journal of Political Economy* in 1949 commemorating the centenary of the publication of "The Communist Manifesto," Schumpeter asserted forcefully that Marx was far more insightful than his classical predecessors in calling attention to the historical achievements of the bourgeoisie. He cites the well-known panegyric by Marx and Engels that culminates in the assertion that the bourgeoisie "during its rule of scarce one hundred years has erected more massive and more colossal productive forces than have all preceding generations together." Earlier economists such as A. Smith and J. S. Mill, Schumpeter adds, never made such extravagant statements concerning "the creative role of the business class." His own generation of economists, Schumpeter also asserted, would "commit the mistake (for such I believe it is) to list as *independent* factors science and technology, whereas Marx's sociology enabled him to see that these as well as 'progress' in such fields as education and hygiene were just as much the products of the bourgeois class culture – hence, ultimately, of the business class – as was the business performance itself." (Quoted above in Chapter 1; the italics here are Schumpeter's.) Thus, Schumpeter asserts his agreement with Marx that science, as well as technology, need to be understood as variables that are responsive to economic forces – i.e., they are endogenous.[1]

Obviously, to begin with, there are degrees of endogeneity. History does, indeed, matter. No human generation has ever started from scratch. Each generation is necessarily shaped by, and builds upon, a cultural and intellectual inheritance derived from preceding generations. Isaac Newton was explicitly acknowledging this when he stated, of his own remarkable intellectual accomplishments in his theory of gravitational force: "If I have seen further it is by standing on the shoulders of giants." Newton stood firmly on the shoulders of one particular giant, Johannes Kepler, and his theory that all planets move in an elliptical orbit around the sun. In this sense there is always a general restriction upon the notion of complete endogeneity. Indeed, a good reason for studying economic history, in my view, is to understand better the role of such restrictions, as well as the forces leading to their eventual relaxation.

I propose, then, to examine some of the specific forces that account for the increasing endogeneity of both science and technology in the course of the century that has recently drawn to a close. At the same time, I believe that Schumpeter's assertions (especially in Chapter 11 of *Capitalism, Socialism and Democracy*, "The Civilization of Capitalism") that, historically, science and technology need to be understood specifically as creatures of the bourgeois mentality and culture, are too broad-stroked and indiscriminate in nature. The channels of connection in that chapter are, at the very least, not sufficiently spelled out, and his assertions may be subject to the same kinds of strictures as Schumpeter himself addressed to those writers who attributed the historic rise of capitalism to a certain zeitgeist. Moreover, counterexamples spring readily to mind. The huge increase in support for both research and education in science and technology, in the Soviet Union and Japan, can hardly be attributed to a sudden efflorescence of bourgeois culture or commercial incentives.[2]

On the other hand, the alterations in Schumpeter's own views, from his youthful *Theory of Economic Development* to his mature *Capitalism, Socialism and Democracy*, incorporate a recognition of certain institutional changes in western capitalism that had come about in the course of his own lifetime – i.e., roughly, the first forty years of the twentieth century. In his early *Theory of Economic Development* (1911) and even in his later *Business Cycles* (1939), invention is treated as exogenous, as something carried out offstage; at the very least, the rate and direction of inventive activity are not explicitly shaped by economic forces. Schumpeter had very little to say about the determinants of inventive activity until the last decade of his life. At the same time, the actual adoption of inventions – the innovative act – are treated as not only endogenous but as a central fact of Schumpeter's business cycle theory.

By the time *Capitalism, Socialism and Democracy* was published (1942), Schumpeter had come to place considerable emphasis on the economic determinants of invention. Or, more precisely, he argued that both invention and innovation were becoming institutionalized and "automated" in the large corporation, a development that substantially – and successfully – bureaucratized the entrepreneurial function. One might argue that there was a simple reason for Schumpeter's change of view: the capitalist world, about which he was writing, had itself changed drastically in the first forty years or so of the twentieth century, and Schumpeter's later view simply recorded a significant change in capitalist reality.

Why is the economics of science so difficult?

Schumpeter would, I believe, have applauded the emergence of a discipline devoted to the subject of the economics of technological change that has emerged since his death in 1950. In fact, I believe that emergence owed some considerable debt to the influence of Schumpeter himself. I am also confident that he would have been an avid reader of, and perhaps a contributor to, the recent theoretical literature on "endogenous technological change." Indeed, I would argue that both Marx and Schumpeter deserve to be regarded as progenitors of this recent and extremely welcome theoretical innovation, which attempts to construct a rigorous analytical framework for understanding how economies acquire the expanding knowledge base that underlies new technological capabilities.[3] In attempting to illuminate the forces that have been at work in strengthening the endogeneity of technological change, my analysis here can be thought of as standing in a relationship of complementarity to that theoretical literature.[4]

But, although Schumpeter would surely have welcomed the construction of an economics of technological change, he might also have wondered why an economics of science (as opposed to a sociology of science) has taken so long to develop. After all, economics as a discipline has shown some strong imperialistic tendencies in recent decades. It has successfully colonized a number of fields, but it has only just recently begun to colonize science.[5] There has already existed for some time an economics of education, an economics of health, an economics of voting behavior, an economics of marriage, an economics of divorce, and an economics of crime.[6] As some indication of the elevated status of this kind of research, one of its most eminent practitioners, Gary Becker, was awarded a Nobel prize in 1992.

Why, then, has the economics of science taken so long to happen? This question is particularly pertinent in view of what we have long believed about science. It has, after all, been an article of faith, at least as far back as the essays of Francis Bacon, adviser to the first Queen Elizabeth 400 years ago, that scientific research yields huge economic benefits.[7]

A partial answer is that an economic interpretation of scientific activity had long seemed intrinsically far-fetched, or at least implausible. The popular image of the scientist has been that of a remote, and perhaps even eccentric figure, typically absent-minded, rumple dressed, and badly in need of a haircut, who pursued arcane questions not understood by the man in the street, and who was certainly not primarily responding to economic motives. And of course there has always been some truth to this picture. There is plenty of historical evidence – say in Victorian England – of scientists who were independent men of ample financial means, i.e., gentlemen, who were totally committed to the pursuit of seemingly complex questions of no apparent practical import whatever. Darwin is perhaps the best-known specimen of what I have in mind, although his "findings" were controversial in the extreme. Indeed, they still are in "Creationist" circles.

In the course of the twentieth century, along with the sharply rising costs of scientific research and the fact that scientists had become, predominantly, salaried employees in large, hierarchical organizations, not only in universities but also in industrial labs and mission-oriented government agencies, a central sociological fact was lost, and has remained lost, in the literature. That is, there is a vital distinction that needs to be maintained between the motives and priorities of the working scientist and those of the decision makers in the organizations in which they are employed.[8]

Thus, while it may be true of working scientists that they are single-mindedly committed to the goals of "pure" science, decisions to employ or to finance scientists are likely to be based upon a very different set of priorities. Although a distinguished astrophysicist or molecular biologist may be unreservedly committed to the advancement of science, decisions with respect to employment and resource allocation in a large corporation or government agency – including government agencies ostensibly committed to advancing the frontiers of basic science – may quite legitimately be made with more utilitarian goals in mind. There is nothing devious or sinister in any of this. The unsurprising fact is that decisions that determine the size of research budgets for different scientific disciplines are likely to be based on social objectives, and the possibility of economic payoffs are likely to be major components of those objectives.[9] Thus, economic considerations may loom large in the determination of science budgets in both industry and government, and there is no reason why this may not be, at the same time, perfectly compatible with a totally disinterested pursuit of scientific knowledge on the part of employed scientists. Indeed, it is usually highly desirable – i.e., socially functional – that this should be the case.

At the same time, the old stereotype of "disinterestedness" must be handled with care. The term should not be interpreted to mean, as it has often naively been taken to mean, that the scientist has no personal interest – whether ego gratification or pure financial interest – in the eventual outcome of her research. Scientists of course have "interests," and "disinterestedness" in this context ought to mean that personal interests have not improperly shaped the nature of the research findings.

The issue of the reward structure of scientific institutions has been one where economic reasoning has proven rewarding. The work of Robert Merton and other sociologists has shown how the establishment of priority came to play such a major role in scientific discovery. In the community of scientists, as Merton has shown, recognition and enhanced reputation have, for three centuries or so, been the reward for priority in scientific discovery.[10] More recently, Dasgupta and David, building elegantly upon the work of Merton and other sociologists, have shown how the openness of scientific institutions can repair some of the well-known deficiencies of ordinary market incentives in the advancement of scientific knowledge.[11]

Thus, some progress has been made, but there is another partial answer to the question of why an economics of science has taken so long to emerge: economics is a discipline that studies the principles involved in achieving an efficient use of scarce resources. Of course it is possible to construct rigorous formal models of optimal resource allocation in the realm of science. But to provide useful guidance for the allocation of science budgets requires an ability to make some reasonably credible comparison of prospective costs and benefits. Now, we do in fact know how to calculate the costs of linear accelerators, synchrotron radiation machines, Hubble telescopes, the mapping of the human genome, etc. Indeed, not long ago the US Congress decided to cancel the construction of a superconducting supercollider when the estimated costs threatened to escalate up to $11 billion or $12 billion. (In fact, it is costing well over $1.5 billion just to close down the project!)

But while it is relatively straightforward to calculate the costs of conducting Big Science, it remains extraordinarily difficult to calculate the benefits. In fact, there are those who would say that, if you could calculate, ex ante, the benefits of a prospective research project, then the project was, by definition, not science, or at least not basic science. And, if one insists on considering only the narrowly economic benefits, it would be difficult to make any sort of case at all for some of the biggest projects of Big Science. What case could possibly be made for the purely economic benefits of the Hubble Telescope?

It is true that history is full of unexpected benefits that have flowed from scientific research – including research for which no benefits whatever were anticipated at the time the research was undertaken. But the general acknowledgment of the likelihood of unanticipated benefits hardly constitutes a useful guide to the determination of the size of the annual public subsidy to science, or the allocation of a budget of a given size among the many competing possible uses in different fields of science. In a nutshell, the uncertainties concerning the possible benefits of basic scientific research are simply immense. Faraday is reputed to have replied to a member of parliament who skeptically inquired of him what was the use of his discovery of the principles of electromagnetic induction in 1831: "Sir, I do not know, but of one thing I am quite certain: some day you will tax it." And, of course, Faraday was right.

Part of the difficulty is that new scientific knowledge, even after it has been "produced," needs to be thought of, at least in economic terms, as an intermediate good. Such knowledge does not ordinarily enter the market place, and its economic value should presumably be measured as a possible input to a later project that may eventually lead to a marketable product. But this involves, at best, a highly speculative set of conjectures, as Arrow pointed out in a fundamental article many years ago.[12]

The institutionalization of research

The proposition that technological change has become increasingly endogenous in the course of the twentieth century must necessarily lead to an analysis that focuses on a key institutional innovation: the industrial research laboratory. It was these industrial labs that determined the extent to which the activities of the scientific community could be made to be responsive to the needs of the larger society. But such a statement, by itself, is not very illuminating. This is because these research labs, which had their origin in the late nineteenth-century organic chemical industry in Germany, depended for their effective performance upon a network of other institutions. These included, especially, universities that performed two essential functions: (1) they trained scientists and engineers who would eventually take up employment in industrial labs, where they would make a critical contribution to the profitability of industrial research, and (2) they also performed various kinds of disciplinary research that would push out the frontiers of knowledge. The network would also include governments, or other sources, that were prepared to provide subsidies to finance research in areas where it was anticipated that the social returns were likely to be substantially higher than the private returns. In the US, philanthropic foundations, such as the Rockefeller and Carnegie Foundations, have also been particularly significant in the twentieth century.

A central observation here is that, after World War II, most advanced industrial countries vastly increased the funds that they were prepared to commit to the conduct of research, although at significantly differing levels. Furthermore, the industrial labs varied enormously in their importance and effectiveness (1) over the course of time, (2) across national boundaries, and (3) across industrial boundary lines.[13]

The economic role of universities has been so profound that it will have to be explored in more detail in the next chapter. For the present, it needs to be said that the conduct of university research also included the establishment of a number of entirely new disciplines, especially engineering disciplines, that were to assume roles of great economic significance in the conceptualization and the design of new technologies. Of special importance have been electrical engineering, chemical engineering, aeronautical engineering, metallurgy (now "materials sciences") and, more recently, computer science. In the case of the US, at least, the magnitude of expenditures on university research in engineering disciplines has been huge. R&D spending devoted to these disciplines at American universities now far exceeds expenditures devoted to the physical sciences. But far and away the largest recipients are the life sciences which, in 1995, received well over half of all university R&D expenditures. The extent to which the life sciences now dominate university research is a reflection of the vast commitment of the federal government to health-related research. Half of the life sciences research budget of academic institutions is now devoted to the medical sciences.[14]

With respect to industrial research, it is important that the activities of industrial research labs not be judged by academic criteria. The industrial research lab is essentially an institutional innovation in which the research agenda is largely shaped by the changing needs of industrial technologies.[15] The role of industrial scientists and engineers is to improve the performance and reliability of those technologies and to reduce costs, as well as to invent entirely new technologies. Thus, the industrial research lab has had the effect of subjecting science to commercial criteria. In so doing it has rendered science more and more an endogenous activity, whose directions are increasingly shaped by economic forces and concentrated on the achievement of economic goals. Science has become gradually incorporated, in the course of the twentieth century, into a crucial part of the growth system that has propelled industrial societies along their long-term growth trajectories.

That growth system, in which technological change played a central role, is now reinforced in the most advanced industrial countries by a scientific research network that has strong public and private components: (1) large public subsidies to science, such as Germany's Max Planck and Frauenhofer Societies, Italy's National Research Council (CNR), France's CNRS, INSERM, and Institut Pasteur, or America's more than 700 federal labs, which disburse public funds for the achievement of a wide spectrum of national objectives; (2) higher educational institutions that perform substantial amounts of scientific research (albeit with large differences among countries), in addition to their older, well-established training functions; (3) a substantial research commitment in private industry, where scientific resources are specifically directed toward strengthening and expanding a firm's technological capabilities; and (4) a myriad of professional and business associations, whose journals, annual meetings and standing committees provide innumerable opportunities for the exchange of useful information.[16]

But these institutions, however important, are only a part of the story of the forces shaping the thrust of research. The very success of past technological change has been to vastly strengthen the current incentive to commit resources, i.e., R&D funds, to the improvement of technologies that already exist. Insofar as the past performance of a successful economy focuses attention and resources upon products or processes that have been inherited from the past, it seems obvious to say that endogenous forces are at work, i.e., the allocation of R&D expenditures today is being largely shaped by the outcome of economic decisions, and their consequences, that were made at an earlier date. The counterfactual question of how current R&D budgets might be allocated differently in the absence of past successes is impossible to answer beyond stating that those budgets would undoubtedly have been smaller and they would have been allocated in different ways that cannot now be specified.

What is clear, however, is that the vast bulk of what is regarded today as R&D spending involves spending on products that have been around for decades as a result of past economic activities. This observation is confirmed by annual surveys that were conducted over a number of years by McGraw-Hill. These surveys asked the appropriate corporate decision makers to estimate how much of their R&D budgets were devoted to (1) improving products that already exist, as compared to (2) the invention of new products. The response, with a high degree of consistency, was that approximately 80 per cent of R&D expenditures were devoted to improving old products, and only 20 per cent to the invention of new ones. From a different angle we may observe that, for many years, aggregate R&D for the American economy has broken down into one-third R and two-thirds D. And, it is fair to say, the D of R&D is primarily focused upon the improvement of pre-existing products rather than the design of entirely new ones.

Thus, it is inappropriate to think of R&D expenditures as if they were resources that were primarily committed to the search for major breakthrough innovations of the Schumpeterian type. Rather, their main goal is to improve the performance, or reduce the cost, of old technologies. A moment's reflection suggests that this should not be surprising. The transistor, which has so dominated technological change in electronics in the postwar years, is now more than fifty years old, having been invented in December 1947. The automobile has been around for one hundred years, and the airplane is within a few years of its centenary. Yet transportation equipment is the largest sector of the American economy when sectors are ranked by company-financed R&D, and these two "old" transportation forms absorb the great bulk of those expenditures. The camera is 150 years old, and the Fourdrinier machine, which is the mainstay of the paper-making industry today, was patented during the Napoleonic Wars, yet both technologies continue to be the objects of significant research and improvement. The generation of electricity for commercial purposes is usually dated from the year 1882, when the Pearl Street station, on the lower end of the island of Manhattan, began to offer electricity to customers. This event set the stage for more than a century of R&D involving, for the most part, individually small improvements in the modification of boiler design, the introduction of alloys of higher performance, pulverization of the coal, and a rise in operating pressures and temperatures over many decades. Although only specialists would be able to identify more than a few of the innumerable improvements, the amount of coal required to generate a kilowatt-hour of electricity had declined by almost an order of magnitude between the early twentieth century and the 1960s. The cumulative effects of individually small improvements in the generation of electric power, carried out over a sufficiently long period of time on what is now called a general purpose technology (GPT),[17] have transformed the world economy.

The telephone has been around for well over one hundred years, but its performance has recently been enhanced by facsimile transmission, electronic mail (e-mail), voice mail, cellular phones, conferences calls and "800" numbers. One may respond that some of these "enhancements" really deserve to be regarded as the invention of major new products, rather than a mere improvement upon old ones. I would not be inclined to disagree, but I would insist that the "old" product, the standard telephone, was the technological platform on which the more recent products were built. That is to say, what we are observing is a process in which successful earlier investments in inventive activities have created economic incentives that have generated many years of further investment in product improvement. These later investments, which now appear to dominate the R&D budgets of advanced capitalist economies, are thus clearly endogenous in their nature.

How engineering disciplines have shaped science

Up until now, in examining aspects of the R&D process, I have not distinguished with particular sharpness between the scientific "R" component, and the more purely technological, or engineering, development ("D") component. In modern societies, science and technology are intimately intertwined. That intertwining is itself a big subject that I cannot enter into here in a systematic way, but is one that I have discussed elsewhere.[18] For present purposes, however, several points need to be made.

The first point is this. The development of engineering disciplines has, historically, exercised a powerful effect in the industrial world on the incentive to undertake research of a scientific nature. And here it must be pointed out that, in recent years, industrial firms have accounted for a large and rising fraction of the economy's scientific research, the R of R&D. Moreover, even if we focus exclusively on the narrow category of basic research alone, the National Science Foundation (NSF) reports that, in recent years, more than 25 per cent of basic research in the US has been funded by industrial firms. It is reasonable to assume that privately financed basic research would not be undertaken in the absence of the prospect of some economic payoff, although that payoff need not necessarily be defined in terms of a solution to a problem internal to the firm. It may, instead, constitute the necessary "table-stakes" for monitoring research taking place outside the firm, especially in universities, in federal labs or in competing firms. Effective monitoring, in other words, may require a considerable internal competence to comprehend and to evaluate what goes on in the larger research world outside.[19]

What role, then, is played by engineering disciplines in determining the scientific agenda of individual firms? The development of engineering disciplines, first of all, serves to raise the prospective payoff to research of a more purely scientific nature. The reason for this is that it is these engineering disciplines that offer the possibility of converting the findings of scientific research into marketable products. It is the existence of these engineering disciplines, then, that has powerfully strengthened the endogeneity of science in advanced capitalist economies. Although it is common to characterize engineering disciplines as being essentially applied science, a more careful unwinding of the intertwining of science and technology suggests that – not surprisingly – the willingness of profit-seeking firms to devote money to scientific research is very much influenced by the prospect of converting research findings into finished products. The actual conduct of scientific research may not be undertaken with specific objectives in mind, but rather with an increased confidence that, whatever the specific research findings, a well-developed engineering capability will increase the likelihood of using these findings to bring improved or new products to the market place. From this perspective, there is a serious sense in which the economist may argue that the science of chemistry should be thought of as an application of chemical engineering!

This argument seems particularly pertinent to the specialty of polymer chemistry. In the US, at least, polymer chemistry is a field that was dominated by the industrial research community for many years. The fundamental research contributions of Wallace Carothers at the du Pont Corporation, beginning in 1928, owed a great deal to the increasing maturity of chemical engineering – itself a discipline to which du Pont had made important contributions.[20] Carothers' major scientific research findings resulted in the discovery of nylon, the first of the synthetic fibers. However, a gigantic development effort was required, involving an intense concentration of effort on the part of chemical engineers over a period of eleven years, before the first pair of nylon stockings became available. It is doubtful that du Pont would have committed itself to the fundamental researches in polymer chemistry in the absence of the progress in chemical engineering in the decade preceding 1927. This progress in an engineering discipline strengthened the firm's confidence that it would be able to convert the findings of scientific research expenditures into commercializable products.

How technological breakthroughs shape science

The final argument with respect to the growing endogeneity of scientific research goes beyond the role played by engineering disciplines in strengthening the incentives to perform scientific research. The argument here is that the development of a new technology of considerable commercial significance, regardless of the origins of that technology, may provide, and often has provided, a powerful stimulus to systematic scientific research. This proposition is surprising only if one is already committed to a rigid, linear view of the innovation process, one in which causality is always expected to run from prior scientific research to "downstream" product design and engineering development. There is, in fact, a straightforward, endogenous explanation. A major technological breakthrough typically provides a powerful signal that a new set of profitable opportunities has been opened up in some precisely identified location. Consequently, it is understood that scientific research that can lead to further improvements in that new technology may turn out to be highly profitable.

This kind of dependence, in which prior technological breakthroughs give rise to scientific research, is not, of course, a uniquely twentieth-century phenomenon. It can be seen in the spectacular developments in the iron and steel industry that began in the 1850s. In the cases of the three great innovations in the second half of the nineteenth century – the Bessemer converter, Siemens' open-hearth furnace, and the Gilchrist-Thomas basic lining that made possible the exploitation of high phosphorus ores – none of them drew upon chemical knowledge that was less than half a century old. However, adoption of these innovations dramatically raised the payoffs resulting from the acquisition of new scientific knowledge concerning the properties of steel.[21]

The very success of the Bessemer process in lowering the price of steel, and in introducing it into a rapidly expanding array of new uses, made it necessary to subject the inputs of the process to quantitative chemical analysis. This was because, as was quickly discovered, the quality of steel, and its structural integrity, were highly sensitive to even minute variations in the composition of the inputs. Phosphorus, it turned out, had an immediate and very deleterious effect upon the quality of the final product. Furthermore, the addition of even minute quantities of nitrogen from the air during the course of the brief Bessemer blast led eventually to serious and unexpected deterioration in the performance of the metal, as in the case of steel rails, although this causal relationship was not established until many years later. Indeed, it is fair to say that the present-day subject of materials science had its origins in the need to solve these very practical questions with respect to the behavior of metals that were associated with the emergence of the modern steel industry in the second half of the nineteenth century.

But some even deeper issues pertaining to the question of endogeneity were involved here. The research that was stimulated by the failure of Bessemer's original "acid" process eventually led to the identification of the "culprit": it was determined that even small amounts of phosphorus in the iron ore rendered the pig iron produced with such ore unusable. By contrast, the Gilchrist-Thomas "basic" process, announced in 1879, neutralized the deleterious effects of phosphorus, and was applicable to both the Bessemer and the later open-hearth processes. But the basic process was also a technological change of enormous geopolitical as well as economic significance because it made possible the utilization of continental Europe's immense deposits of high phosphorus iron ores (minette ores).

Reverting to the larger theme of this chapter, the point that needs to be made here is not only that technological change is endogenous, but that the same is true of the raw material inputs that are employed in the productive process. The research that led to the later basic process made possible a gigantic expansion of the iron and steel industry's resource base. Thus, a very simple chemical insight, that the addition of lime would result in the removal of phosphorus from molten iron, had led to a vast enlargement of the resource supply of a major industry.[22]

The point is a general one and is by no means confined to metallurgy in the nineteenth century. The use of the electric arc furnace in the second half of the twentieth century has transformed discarded metals – scrap or, more colloquially, junk – into a valuable material input for the steel industry. The electric furnace is capable of functioning with a 100 per cent scrap charge and, indeed, all of the new steel-making capacity of the American steel industry since 1970 has consisted of such mini-mills, as these electric furnaces are now called. The electric arc furnace is also used in the recycling of aluminum, a process that requires only about 5 per cent of the energy requirements of aluminum production when beginning with bauxite ores.[23]

At the beginning of the twentieth century the American wood-pulp industry utilized only the spruce and fir trees of the northern portions of the country. Improvements in sulphate pulping technology in the 1920s made possible the exploitation of the faster growing southern pine, which was previously unusable. As a result of this new technology (which had its origin in Sweden), the American south accounted for over half of the country's woodpulping capacity by the mid-1950s, a major redefinition of the economy's resource base.[24] Recently, Paul David and Gavin Wright have provided documentation for the argument that America's position as the world's leading mineral-producing nation was not an exogenous fact of "Nature."

> Minerals with economic value do indeed occur unevenly across the surface of the earth, but between 1850 and 1950, the United States exploited its resource potential to a far greater extent than other countries of the world. The abundance of American natural resources did not derive exclusively from geological endowment . . . but reflected the intensity of search, technologies of extraction, refining, and utilization; market development and transportation costs; and legal, institutional and political structures affecting all of these.[25]

In other words, the material inputs going into blast furnaces, into mini-mills, into paper mills and into a wide range of mineral-using productive processes, all need to be regarded as endogenous.

World War II represented a major turning point for the organization of the American economy and the role played by the federal government. After the war the federal government became the patron of scientific research on a scale that was without earlier precedent, either in the US or in any other country.[26]

It is important to remember how recent in history is US world leadership in scientific research. That leadership became apparent only in the years after 1945. New institutions, such as the National Science Foundation, were established, and some existing institutions, such as the National Institutes of Health, were vastly expanded. The exigencies of the Cold War led to a massive enlargement in the military demand for highly sophisticated technologies. Vast amounts of money in support of science and engineering flowed to the universities, and the GI Bill of Rights, which financed higher education for returning veterans, brought a profusion of highly skilled professionals into the postwar economy.

In the years following World War II the association of certain industries with organized research has become so common that the neologism "high tech" has been coined as a shorthand expression in referring to them. Industrial research labs experienced a considerable expansion in the postwar years, and by 1992 there were very nearly 12,000 of them in the US.[27] Research at these laboratories was powerfully shaped by the need to improve the effectiveness of the technology upon which the firm depended – indeed, that was their raison d'être. A number of these labs have not only applied scientific knowledge to industrial purposes; they have also been generating some of that knowledge by performing research of the highest quality. Nobel prizes have been received by scientists working at Bell Labs and at IBM, even though they worked in a context where the overall research agenda was oriented toward the improvement of specific advanced technological systems. The problems encountered by sophisticated industrial technologies, and the anomalous observations and unexpected difficulties that they have encountered, have served as powerful stimuli to much fruitful scientific research in the academic community as well as the industrial research laboratory. In these ways the responsiveness of scientific research to economic needs and technological opportunities has been powerfully reinforced.[28]

This was dramatically demonstrated in the case of the advent of the transistor, which was announced in 1948. Within a decade of that event, solid-state physics, which had previously attracted the attention of only a small number of researchers and was not even taught at most universities, had been transformed into the largest subdiscipline of physics. It was the development of the transistor that changed that situation by dramatically upgrading the potential payoff to research in the solid state. J. A. Morton, who headed the fundamental development group that was formed at Bell Laboratories after the invention of the transistor, reported that it was extremely difficult to hire people with a knowledge of solid-state physics in the late 1940s.[29] Moreover, it is important to emphasize that the rapid mobilization of intellectual resources to perform research in the solid state occurred in the university community as well as in private industry, immediately after the announcement of the momentous findings of Shockley and his research colleagues at Bell Labs.[30]

The chronology of the events referred to is essential to my argument. Transistor technology was not the eventual consequence of a huge prior build-up of resources devoted to solid-state physics, although it was of course true that some of the twentieth century's most creative physicists had been devoting their considerable energies to the subject. Rather, it was the initial breakthrough of the transistor, as a functioning piece of hardware, that set into motion a vast subsequent commitment of scientific resources. The difficulties that Shockley encountered with the operation of the early point-contact transistors led him into a systematic search for a deeper explanation of their behavior in terms of the underlying quantum physics of semiconductors. This search not only led eventually to a vastly superior amplifying device, the junction transistor, but also contributed to a more profound understanding of the science of semiconductors. Indeed, Shockley's famous and highly influential book, *Electrons and Holes in Semiconductors*, drew heavily upon this research, and was the direct outgrowth of an in-house course that Shockley had taught for Bell Labs' personnel. Shockley even ran a six-day course at Bell Labs in June 1952 for professors from some thirty universities as part of an attempt to encourage the establishment of university courses in transistor physics. Clearly, the main flow of scientific knowledge during this period was from industry to university, and not the other way around. Indeed, for a considerable period of time, Stanford University and the University of California at Berkeley had to employ scientists from local industry to teach courses in solid-state physics.[31]

A similar sequence can be seen in the commitment of resources to surface chemistry, after problems with the reliability of early transistors pointed in that direction. More recently, and to compress a more complex chain of events, the development of laser technology suggested the feasibility of using optical fibers for telephone transmission purposes. This possibility naturally pointed to the field of optics, where advances in scientific knowledge could now be expected to have potentially high economic payoffs. As a result, optics as a field of scientific research experienced a great resurgence in the 1960s and after. It was converted by changed expectations, based upon past and prospective technological innovations, from a relatively quiet intellectual backwater of science into a burgeoning field of research.[32]

I draw the conclusion from this examination that, under modern industrial conditions, technology has come to shape science in the most powerful of ways: by playing a major role in determining the research agenda of science as well as the volume of resources devoted to specific research fields. One could examine these relationships in much finer detail by showing how, throughout the high tech sectors of the economy, shifts in the technological needs of industry have brought with them associated shifts in emphasis in scientific research. When, for example, the semiconductor industry moved from a reliance upon discrete circuits (transistors) to integrated circuits, there was also a shift from mechanical to chemical methods of fabrication. When Fairchild Semiconductors began to fabricate integrated circuits, they did so by employing new methods of chemical etching that printed the transistors in the silicon wafers and also laid down the tracks between them. This chemical technique did away with much expensive wiring, and also produced integrated circuits that operated at much higher speeds. At the same time, the increased reliance upon chemical methods brought with it an increased attention to the relevant subfields of chemistry.

I cite the experience of changing methods of wafer fabrication to indicate the ways in which the changing needs and priorities of industry have provided the basis for new priorities in the world of scientific research. But it is essential to emphasize that these new priorities exercised their influence, not only upon the world of industrial research, but upon the conduct of research within the university community as well. I need only point out that Stanford University has its own Center for Integrated Systems. This Center, according to the university bulletin, "is a laboratory joining government and industrially funded research on microelectronic materials, devices, and systems . . . In addition, CIS provides start-up research funds and maintains a 'Fellow–Mentor' program with industry."[33]

Of course my analysis of the endogeneity of science has been no more than the sketch that is permitted in a single chapter, and the same is true of the earlier sketch of the endogeneity of technology. Moreover, entire categories of influence of technology upon science have been completely ignored here, such as the massive impact of instrumentation, i.e., technologies of observation and measurement.[34] All these subjects deserve far more attention by economists and economic historians who are interested in endogeneity, not only as a theoretical modeling exercise, but also as an empirical phenomenon of growing significance throughout the entire course of the twentieth century.

Chapter 3

American universities as endogenous institutions

Introduction

Universities, of course, perform a variety of functions, but my main interest in our present context is in the role universities play as producers and transmitters of economically useful knowledge, by which I mean primarily technological knowledge. More specifically, I want to suggest that American universities differ from those of other countries in the greater speed and greater extent of their response to changing economic circumstances. In characterizing them in such fashion, I mean to suggest that there is much about their behavior that can be understood as endogenous, or at least as a good deal more endogenous than the universities of other countries. I want to examine them, then, from a comparative international perspective, even, to some extent, from an industrial organization (IO) perspective. Perhaps a more appropriate title for this chapter, then, would be "American universities: structure and performance."

Given this very ambitious undertaking, it will be necessary to make some broad, sweeping comparisons of the organizational structure and performance of universities in continental Europe and the US; and therefore I will obviously be painting with a very broad brush, on both sides of the Atlantic. After that I will suggest some connections between certain organizational features of American higher education and the success of American universities as economic institutions. In the context of this chapter, my focus will be mainly on those subjects that are most directly pertinent to technological change, i.e., engineering and science, and my interest will be primarily on the graduate or professional levels at the country's research-oriented universities.

I should also confess, at the outset, that this chapter represents, for me, an initial foray into a new territory that I intend to explore more intensively in the future.

American universities in comparative perspective

I take it as almost axiomatic that, if one evaluates universities either in terms of intellectual performance or economic impact, American universities in the years since World War II have been spectacularly successful on a world scale. This success might be measured in terms of the award of Nobel prizes and other awards for scientific achievement, or in terms of publications in professional journals, or citation analysis. Or it might be measured in terms of how the most ambitious students overseas vote with their feet when they have had the freedom to choose the country to which they will travel for their graduate or professional training.[1] Or it might be measured in terms of the number of high-tech, start-up firms to which universities have given birth.

American universities, I suggest, would have to be judged to be highly successful by each of these criteria. At the same time, it is essential to remember how recent in history is American world leadership in scientific research. As recently as the outbreak of World War II, the US was far behind Germany, well behind the UK and slightly behind France in terms of the cumulative number of Nobel prizes in science. Indeed, until the early 1930s, when the Nazis came to power, a bright and ambitious young American chemist or physicist would have been strongly urged to go to Germany to do his doctoral research at places like Heidelberg, Leipzig or Göttingen. And the best students did exactly that. Indeed, the very idea that it was an appropriate use of federal tax revenues to support the conduct of basic research in universities is a post World War II notion in the US. In this respect, the period after World War II involved a fundamental transformation in the policies of the US federal government. During this period the federal government became, for the first time, a generous patron of university science, a role that had much to do with the subsequent flowering of science in America.

I would also like to suggest that, if one looks carefully at what goes on at American research universities today, one gets a picture very different from the stylized one, as it is often painted by American academic scientists and their spokesmen in Washington. That usual picture describes American universities as the home of scientists who are single-mindedly pursuing the advancement of fundamental scientific knowledge, with no practical, utilitarian objectives in mind.

Of course, that image is not totally wrong. In America, as opposed to most of Europe, universities are indeed the place where more than half of the country's basic scientific research is conducted.[2] But the image is highly misleading for what it omits. American universities, in reality and not as "ideal types" in the tradition of Max Weber, need to be understood as institutions that have been highly responsive to the economic needs of their society. In fact, I would like to identify this economic responsiveness of American universities as the first, and most basic of several of their distinctive features, when they are examined in a comparative context with European universities. This is the main justification for my assertion that American universities need to be understood as endogenous.

Let me identify the other distinctive features of American universities, as I see them, right away. They are highly decentralized, and very closely connected, they are intensely competitive. So their economic responsiveness has to be seen in the context of a highly competitive environment. Indeed, that competitive environment has been a major *reason*, historically, for such responsiveness.

It should not be necessary to expand much on the competitiveness of American universities. They compete intensely for faculty, who are highly mobile. American professors compete for all sorts of things (not the least of which is parking space!). They compete with one another to a far greater extent than is true in European universities. American faculty compete most intensely for research support. Success at the major research universities depends crucially upon financial support to provide released time from teaching obligations, support for research assistants, and access to specialized equipment or source materials. Such support is likely to be granted through a rigorous, highly selective peer review process, in which financial support is based upon some estimate of the likely payoff in terms of significant research findings.[3] There is far less support of this kind in Europe – i.e., research grants, awarded through a peer review process, that free faculty from some portion of their teaching obligations.

American professors, especially at the graduate level, compete for the best students within the pool of admitted students. Talented graduate students are essential components of an ambitious research and publishing agenda. Universities compete intensely for the most highly qualified students – although providing generous financial support to the most promising students comes into conflict with another goal: maximizing revenue from tuition payments. American universities provide sizeable financial rewards to faculty for winning intellectual races within their respective disciplines, races which commonly have a "winner takes all" quality. In Europe, in my observation, many academic races terminate with the appointment to a full professorship – at which point financial incentives are also likely to come to an end, and the professors are, in effect, merely recognized as having successfully "staked out" a particular intellectual territory that they can claim as their own. It is not easy, for example, to identify the financial incentives to continue to do research and to publish, once an Italian academic has become a full professor. In Italian universities, moreover, the peculiar parochialism prevails that there are financial penalties for receiving a PhD from a foreign university. Seniority is weighted heavily in fixing salaries, and the seniority clock does not begin to tick while a student is studying abroad, although it runs for an advanced Italian student so long as she/he remains at an Italian institution.

A common arrangement on the European continent is that universities receive block grants that cover both teaching and research, often with little opportunity for released time from teaching. A younger faculty person who has done, and is doing, no research whatever is, in many situations, treated no differently than a highly productive colleague. Tenure, moreover, is likely to come early. The incentives to encourage research are weak, especially for faculty who do not aspire to professorial status. But I am painfully aware, at this point, that I am painting with an excessively broad brush, across individual countries as well as across academic disciplines. I should therefore like to record my impression, admittedly based upon limited observation, that research productivity in the "hard" sciences and engineering is more explicitly recognized and rewarded in Europe than in the "softer" disciplines.

Perhaps a useful way of contrasting the competitiveness of the American university system with that found in European countries is to say that, although I have obviously found it difficult to resist the use of the term, the American system is *not* really a system, in the sense that France, Germany or Italy may be said to have higher educational systems. In Europe it is not uncommon for a centralized decision making body (e.g., the Ministry of Education) to determine the salaries of university professors, and to impose a high degree of national uniformity upon that salary structure. In many European countries, of course, professors are civil servants, whose salaries are therefore rigidly structured by the civil service system. This often amounts, as in Italy, to salaries based heavily upon seniority.

Thus, there are very limited possibilities for competition among European universities along the salary dimension. Government ministries (in Germany, the Lander) routinely make decisions not only about budgets but also about appointments,[4] promotions, and even such matters as degree requirements. I certainly would not want to deny that Washington's control of research budgets exercises more than a little influence over what goes on at American universities. This is most especially the case with respect to which fields of research will receive the most financial support. Nevertheless, American universities retain a degree of autonomy in their own affairs – pursuing opportunities for solving their own problems and for building upon their own unique strengths or aspirations – that has no close parallel in most of continental Europe. This autonomy of American universities also holds true of state universities, which have played an enormously creative role since the Civil War.

The state universities in America are of course a big separate subject all by themselves. I wish here to make only a single point. The need to meet competition from a large number of other academic institutions for students, faculty, and research support has been a critical factor that has prevented public, state-supported universities from falling into an inflexible "civil service mode." The essential point about American state universities is not only that there are so many of them, but that all public universities are also in competition with private universities, as well as with other public universities. Thus, in contrast to the civil service mode, there have been multiple sources of experimentation, decision making, innovation and, not least, alternative opportunities for academic employment.

An especially critical way in which American universities have competed is by the frequent introduction of new material into the curriculum – so that the content of courses remains up-to-date in ways that, among other things, may be expected to confer advantages in the labor market upon their graduates. In industrial organization terms, we might say that American universities are characterized by a high rate of new product introduction, or product improvement. A current conspicuous case in point is the intense effort among a number of US business schools to take the lead in incorporating a new specialty, electronic commerce, into their teaching programs. Needless to say, the subject is still "brand new," indeed, so much so that installing it in the curriculum, and even reorganizing the curriculum around this innovation, might seem highly premature; nevertheless, some of America's most distinguished business schools have already entered the competition.[5] I will return to this important issue shortly.

Another distinctive feature of the US university system, which it is easy to take for granted because it is so obvious, is its sheer size. Its great size, in contrast to any of the European countries, is important because it has made it possible to maintain a high degree of specialization and diversity within a very large system. We might even invoke the shade of Adam Smith here, and recall, for its present relevance, the title of Chapter III of Book I of the *Wealth of Nations:* "That the Division of Labour is Limited by the Extent of the Market." But it should be added that the market for higher education in the US has been so large, not only because of the large population of the country, but also because America has, throughout the twentieth century, admitted a higher percentage of the college age cohort to universities than have European countries. That difference has narrowed considerably in the past thirty years, but it is still substantial.

The American university system, because of its large size, has been able to channel students into institutions that operate according to different academic standards and provide different kinds of education directed toward different goals.[6] A small number of elite institutions in the US (the top twenty-five or so) can "cream off" the most talented students, while a wide range of institutions are available to accommodate the varying needs of the less talented, the less well-prepared, or the less ambitious. The State of California has an explicit three-tier system. Anyone with a high school diploma, or its equivalent, can find a place somewhere within this system, although not necessarily at Berkeley or UCLA.

There is, however, an additional feature of the California system as well as many other American universities, at the undergraduate level, that is worth noticing. It is not only possible to transfer from a community college to a state college, or from either to the top-ranked universities, if grades are good enough, but also to transfer accumulated credits. This possibility encourages upward mobility as well as keeping the doors open for "late bloomers."

I should insert a qualification here. I appealed earlier to the large size of the United States to explain the diversity of academic standards that have been maintained at the university level. That kind of argument cannot, of course, be applied at the level of educational institutions that are operated by state governments. Although California has a population well in excess of 30 million, Wyoming has about one half million, and several states have less than a million. Obviously, then, the highly articulated differences in academic standards that continue to prevail in American post-secondary education cannot be entirely accounted for by the large size of the country's overall population. Other forces must also have been at work.

In some ways the most interesting feature of higher education in America is the last. The American higher educational system has brought about a unique synthesis of advanced research with graduate and professional education. This synthesis has been made possible by the fact that scientific research in the US is heavily concentrated in universities. In Europe, by contrast, universities generally play a far less important role, and specialized scientific research institutes, often with no close connections to the educational process, are much more important.

What can be said about the economics of these arrangements? It is useful to think of graduate students as making an investment in their human capital. Suppose we also distinguish between old science and new science. In the US, the curriculum is being continually updated through the research process, and graduate students, particularly in their role as research assistants, participate directly in activities that place them at the research frontiers of their discipline. They are active participants in frontier research, albeit in a junior role, as apprentices. Consequently, advanced students at American universities are acquiring relatively more new science, science that presumably has a higher market value than the older science that is being acquired by European postgraduate students. This is reflected in the evidence that there is a higher rate of return to investment in human capital at American universities.[7]

Some contrasts with continental Europe

In continental Europe the pattern of specialization has been very different. In particular, there has been a much greater degree of separation between teaching and research. A higher proportion of

European scientific research is performed away from the universities, at specialized research institutes that have historically had little involvement in teaching. In Germany, basic research is heavily concentrated in the various Max Planck Gesellschaften which have had, until recently, little connection with university education. In postwar Eastern Europe practically no advanced research has been conducted in universities. Each country has had its various national academies of science, whose members do most of the serious scientific research, and who have been heavily insulated from any teaching responsibilities. This separation has been especially damaging in Russia, where it is reported to be not uncommon in universities to find scarcely anyone who can lecture knowledgeably about current frontier research in major fields of science.[8]

In France, three large public agencies, CNRS (National Center for Scientific Research), CEA (Energy Commission), and INSERM (National Institute for Health and Medical Research) control the great bulk of scientific research, most of which has, in the past, been spent in-house. But they now also dispense research funds to universities through jointly operated laboratories. The best scientific research has been carried out at a few very distinguished research centers, such as the Institut Pasteur. France has also had the additional complication that many of the very best students do not go to the universities, but to the highly prestigious "Grandes Ecoles" where a rigorous, primarily undergraduate education has prepared an elite for high levels of administrative and engineering responsibilities. Many of these schools have developed distinguished research programs in the engineering and physical sciences over the past two decades.

Of course, the two previous paragraphs have overstated the sharpness of the separation between the research institutes and the universities. The European institutes, to begin with, are "fed" by the universities, since new entrants to the institutes were trained at the universities. In France, the rigorous training, especially in mathematics, that is acquired at the various Grandes Ecoles (e.g., the Ecole Polytechnique) is an important contributor to the high quality of science at the various CNRS institutes and elsewhere. Moreover, research scientists who have distinguished themselves through their research at various European research institutes will often join university faculties, but often only at a later stage in their careers. This is a widely practiced sequence in Germany, where a scientist will apply to join the professoriate after spending a number of years conducting his research in one of the Max Planck Gesellschaften.

A useful way of interpreting the different arrangements between the US and Europe is to say that the American system has exploited the strong complementarities that have existed when teaching and research are performed by the same persons. In one sense, it can be said that the American system is less specialized, in that the same people typically perform two functions whereas, in Europe, one group specializes in teaching and the other group specializes in research. A key argument that can be made for the superiority of the American system is that teaching is better, i.e., it has more valuable content, when it is performed by faculty who are also seriously committed to scientific research, and when, additionally, advanced students actually participate in this research as part of their graduate education. I am also prepared to speculate that the quality of research is better in a system that is less hierarchical and authoritarian than many of those in continental Europe, and where graduate students are encouraged to be critical of authority and to express their disagreements freely.

Thus, I believe that the complementarity between teaching and research cuts both ways: teaching is better when delivered by research-oriented faculty, and research is better when it is carried out in association with advanced students in an intellectual environment that encourages the criticism of authority figures. Moreover, I would also speculate that the American arrangement, in which faculty are required to lecture to classes of bright, attentive, and highly motivated graduate students, has had a nontrivial effect in raising the level of rigor and systematic thinking on the part of the professoriate. Since, until recently at least, European advanced degrees included very little lecturing to more mature students, European faculty have been unable to derive what I would regard as the considerable benefit of prolonged exposure to such audiences.

Suppose that, in the US, the teaching of science consists of 90 per cent old science and 10 per cent new science. In many contexts, both academic and commercial, the 10 per cent new science will be critical. This new knowledge is more likely to be diffused, and to be diffused more rapidly, through teaching in the US than in countries where scientific research is concentrated in special institutes, often remote from the universities, and where students consequently receive much less training in recently acquired scientific knowledge.

As a result, both the private and social payoffs to graduate and professional education are likely to be higher in the US.

The prominent role played by American universities in the high-tech sectors of the economy since World War II is, in my view, closely connected to these distinctive features of advanced graduate education in the US. These features have been especially critical in such new fields as microelectronics, computer science, and biotechnology,[9] fields where, I think it is fair to say, Europe has continued to lag behind the US.[10]

Innovating in the curriculum

This line of reasoning has led me to become particularly interested in the role played by American universities in achieving a rapid rate of diffusion of potentially useful new knowledge. Part of this is, of course, a well-known story. The Morrill Act of 1862 established a system of land-grant colleges which, together with the later introduction of agricultural experiment stations, provided a basic infrastructure for both the transmission of knowledge and the generation of new knowledge at the local (state) level. A key feature of these arrangements was the county agent, who played a crucial role in bringing new information to individual farmers, such as new seed varieties, but who also provided an important feedback mechanism by identifying problems and concerns of farmers at the county level and bringing them to the attention of the agricultural specialists at the state colleges.

The state universities have been, without question, one of the great institutional innovations in the history of American research and education. Many of the early contributions to the applied sciences were carried out at the state universities and the agricultural experiment stations that were associated with these universities. This was the case with respect to one of the great agricultural innovations of the century: hybrid corn. Hybrid corn and the study of genetics were developed at the University of Connecticut Agricultural Experiment Station in the 1920s and at Iowa State University in the 1930s. The nature of the technological changes that issued from these agricultural experiment stations, lodged in state universities, can be readily understood in endogenous terms. The choice of research topics was almost always strongly influenced by economic considerations, as Theodore Schultz pointed out in 1953.[11]

If we consider the technological needs of manufacturing, the history has been more complex, and it needs to be examined in terms of the several different engineering disciplines that emerged to deal with the specific needs of different industrial sectors. A central point about the American scene, over the past century or more, is that universities quickly came to play a key role as the locus of development of new engineering disciplines. In the context of international comparisons, an intriguing point is that US universities several times played a leadership role in developing the useful engineering applications for a newly emerging technology or industry, even when European countries – mainly Germany – were the international leaders in the underlying basic science. This was especially the case in chemical engineering and aeronautical engineering. Chemical engineering is especially interesting because, in the first forty years of the twentieth century, Germany was overwhelmingly the dominating country in the science of chemistry. America's receipt of Nobel prizes in chemistry, compared to the major European powers, tells much of the story. Up to 1939, only three Americans were awarded Nobel prizes in chemistry, compared to fifteen for Germany and six apiece for the UK and France. Between 1940 and 1994, thirty-six Americans received the chemistry prize; the UK was second with seventeen, Germany third with eleven, and France received just one.[12]

But regardless of where the new knowledge was produced, intellectual innovations were introduced into US universities with remarkable speed, where they were further systematized and entered into the teaching curriculum as soon as their potential utility became apparent. Of course, the speed with which intellectual novelties were introduced is one of the most important forms of inter-university competition, as was mentioned earlier. When the economic importance of electricity became obvious, with the introduction of the dynamo in 1882, a new institution, MIT, offered its first course in electrical engineering in the very same year (MIT held its first classes in 1865). By the outbreak of World War I, MIT's electrical engineering department "was reputed to be the best in the world for both technical expertise and the training of potential managers."[13] Cornell University followed suit in 1883 and awarded the first doctorate in the US in the subject as early as 1885. One survey of the beginnings of electrical engineering education in the US states, perhaps with some exaggeration, that "every respectable school – and many seeking respect – had instituted some sort of instruction in the new science."[14] In general, the land-grant state universities of the Midwest moved into this new discipline with greater enthusiasm than the elite eastern universities; there "were in fact almost 20 schools with course enrollments of over 50 in 1897."[15]

The histories of other engineering disciplines, including, more recently, computer science, are broadly similar.[16] Consider the discipline of aeronautical engineering. Aircraft design became a subject of major importance in the second decade of the twentieth century. Germany completely dominated the underlying science, the field of aerodynamics, under the towering leadership of Ludwig Prandtl at Göttingen University – Prandtl was a professor at Göttingen from 1904 until his death in 1953. His articulation of the boundary-layer hypothesis in 1904 was to become one of the fundamental concepts of aerodynamic theory, a theory that was further elaborated primarily in Germany. Nevertheless, in the interwar period it was the Americans, and not the Germans, who excelled in aeronautical engineering and its application to aircraft design.

As early as 1913 MIT began its program in aeronautical engineering when Jerome Hunsaker, at the time an assistant naval constructor at the Boston Navy Yard, went to MIT "to teach a special series of courses in aerodynamics for Navy officers."[17] In 1916, William Durand and Everett Lesley, professors of mechanical engineering at Stanford University, began a study of the optimal shapes of airplane propellers that was to last until 1926, and was to exercise a powerful influence on airplane designers in Europe as well as the US.[18]

Of course, World War I and its turbulent postwar aftermath had a great deal to do with Germany's failure to fully exploit its early leadership in aerodynamics. And it was the darkening cloud of political extremism and virulent anti-Semitism that encouraged Prandtl's most distinguished student, Theodore von Karman, to accept an invitation to join the faculty of California Institute of Technology in Pasadena in 1930.[19] Still, it is far from clear that the sophisticated aerodynamic concepts developed at Göttingen would have had as rapid an application to commercial aircraft design in the German university as it did at Cal Tech, even if the times and the circumstances had been more propitious. Prandtl regarded his research as applied physics rather than engineering, and it is doubtful that he would, himself, have participated in the very practical aircraft design exercises that von Karman became involved in at Cal

Tech, beginning in 1932. Such practical applications were typically regarded as beneath the dignity of a German university professor.[20]

Von Karman, a physicist and mathematician like his teacher Prandtl, joined several of his Cal Tech colleagues in undertaking research directed toward the improvement of aircraft design. This research was fed directly into a design for the nearby Douglas Aircraft Company that was embodied in the prototype DC-1. Two hundred test runs of the DC-1 model were undertaken in Cal Tech's 10-foot wind tunnel. The DC-2 became Douglas's first production, of which 130 were made and, in 1935, the DC-3 entered production. This plane quickly became the dominant design of the world commercial aircraft industry. It was a 21-passenger, two-engine airplane, which carried 80 per cent of America's airline traffic by 1940. Over the succeeding years 11,000 of these aircraft were produced, making it easily the most popular commercial airplane in history, and establishing the United States as the pre-eminent leader in the commercial aircraft industry. The plane directly incorporated a number of the design and structural features of Cal Tech's five aerodynamicists, including von Karman.[21]

To move beyond engineering, it was no accident that the extremely useful subject of statistics was much more widely diffused in the US before World War II, and acquired curriculum and departmental status there well before this happened in Europe. This was so in spite of the fact that the first chair in the subject of statistics was established at University College London, in 1933, and the field of statistics was far more advanced in Britain than the US before World War II. Nor was it an accident that pioneering roles in introducing statistics were played by Iowa State University and the University of North Carolina. Both Iowa and North Carolina had strong agricultural experiment stations where sophisticated statistical analysis was essential in evaluating the results of trial experiments with new crop varieties. Statistics, an obviously useful subject, was readily accepted into departmental status in the US. The first such department was in the University of North Carolina in Chapel Hill. Harold Hotelling, the distinguished mathematical statistician and economist, was persuaded to leave Columbia University and move to the University of North Carolina in 1946 when that university agreed to establish a separate statistics department, the first such in the United States.[22] On the European continent, by contrast, statistics was long regarded as an applied subject that did not deserve the status associated with being taught at a university. The great British statistician and biologist, R. A. Fisher, also spent much of his professional life at an agricultural research station – Rothamsted – where he did some of his most important work on experimental design based on randomization as well as statistical estimation theory. His first academic appointment at University College London, was in the bogus science of eugenics, although his final appointment, at Cambridge, was in genetics.

American universities produce prototypes

I now turn, briefly, to the central role played by American universities in developing what many consider to be the most important innovation of the past half century: the computer. The basic point that I want to make about the computer, in the specific context of this chapter, is that the hardware as well as the software (using the term "software" loosely) was the product of university conceptualization, research, design, and assembly. The stylized view, frequently encountered, that the American university's contribution to innovation terminates long before an innovation has reached the prototype stage, is simply incorrect in the case of the computer and, I would argue, in many other cases as well. The first digital electronic computer, the ENIAC, was brought to the full stage of a working prototype at the Moore School of Electrical Engineering at the University of Pennsylvania, in the fall of 1945. Admittedly it was built during the unusual, forced march conditions of wartime, under a contract with the Aberdeen Proving Grounds in Maryland, which was anxious to improve the accuracy of their ballistics tables. Nevertheless, the machine was essentially a more powerful version of something called the differential analyzer, an analog machine that had been built and operated in the still peaceful early 1930s at MIT under the direction of Vannevar Bush.[23]

In the case of the computer, moreover, American universities not only designed and assembled the initial hardware of the computer industry; they created an entirely new discipline, of huge economic importance, along with the research infrastructure that had to be built in order to exploit the vast potential of the new hardware. It is interesting to note that the discipline is called "computer science," but it is usually lodged in schools of engineering. Research in this new field was primarily financed in its early years by ARPA (Advanced Research Projects Agency of the Pentagon), but it also received some funding from the NSF, including $85 million that went to more than 200 universities between 1957 and 1972 for the purchase of computer hardware. Unlike the NSF, which distributed its support broadly, ARPA focused its support in just a few leading research universities: Carnegie-Mellon, MIT, Stanford, and the University of California at Berkeley.

Here again I want specifically to call attention to the remarkable speed with which the university curriculum was expanded to accommodate an economic (and, after the 1957 Soviet launching of Sputnik, of course also a strategic) need. There were essentially no formal programs in computer science in American universities in 1959 but, within six years, in 1965, there were at least fifteen universities that offered doctorates in the subject and seventeen that offered bachelor's degrees. According to one survey, by the early 1980s computer science had become an extremely popular subject in universities. In 1983 "25,000 bachelor's degrees were awarded in Computer Science, compared with 18,000 in Electrical Engineering, 11,000 in Chemistry, 12,600 in Mathematics and Statistics, and 3,800 in Physics."[24]

It would be possible to examine the process by which American university research, with federal funding, produced a series of innovations in software, computer architecture, and computer networking that led from the ARPANET to the NSFNET which, in turn, came to underpin national and international electronic mail. Today's global communications network, "Internet," traces its origins directly back to the undertaking by ARPANET to link more closely together the activities of four universities, each of which was, at the time, performing research for the Department of Defense. American universities brought Internet all the way to, and even beyond, the prototype stage. In fact, the remarkable degree of openness and accessibility that characterizes today's Internet and World Wide Web must surely owe a great deal to the fact that they were developed primarily in a university context. It is unlikely that this technology would have developed as it has, and as quickly as it has, if it had originated in a commercial environment dominated by proprietary considerations.

American universities should no longer be thought of as institutions that are confined to pushing out the envelope of fundamental science and leaving prototype development to the private sector. Indeed, I have suggested that such a characterization has never been more than, at best, a caricature. American universities produce prototypes.

With respect to medical technology, Academic Medical Centers (AMCs) bear a large responsibility for the development of the main diagnostic imaging technologies that have emerged since the 1950s: the fiber optic endoscope, the CT scanner, and Magnetic Resonance Imaging (MRI). Each of these imaging technologies was brought to the working prototype stage within the university community – in this case, within the Anglo-American university community. The fiber optic endoscope was brought from the initial conceptualization to the prototype stage by a young South African gastroenterologist at the University of Michigan medical school, working closely with an assistant professor of physics and an undergraduate.[25] The CT scanner and MRI, both of which are totally dependent upon the computer, were the joint products of university medical research in the US and UK. Medical research groups at the universities of Nottingham and Aberdeen in Great Britain, along with an improbable participant, Electrical and Musical Industries Ltd (EMI), played key roles in the case of the CT scanner. EMI first marketed the CT scanner and, indeed, managed to dominate that market briefly in the mid-1970s, but then quickly went bankrupt. Allan Cormack of Tufts University (Massachusetts) and Godfrey Hounsfield of EMI shared the Nobel prize in medicine and physiology in 1979 for their contributions to the invention of the CT scanner. Hounsfield designed the instrumentation for image reconstruction and Cormack developed the equations that made image reconstruction possible. On the American side, medical participants from UCLA, Georgetown University, and various branches of the State University of New York were prominent participants in the new diagnostic technologies. A feature common to both the American and British scenes was the close cooperation, at both the R and D stages, between the medical school and the physics department of each university. A similar story could be told with respect to MRI. Raymond Damadian (significantly, an assistant professor of biophysics as well as a physician at the Downstate Medical Center in New York, part of the SUNY system) took out an early patent on MRI in 1974.[26]

The connection between physics and medicine was not, of course, without distinguished historical precedent: Roentgen, who discovered the diagnostic capabilities of X-rays in 1895, was a professor of physics at the University of Würzberg, and the winner of the first Nobel prize in physics.

Clearly it is necessary to redefine the role of US universities as economic institutions. They have, for the past century and a half, been far more active participants in the economic arena, and more responsive to the changing economic needs of the larger society, than those in Europe. They have been deeply involved, in the postwar years, in prototype development in a number of high-tech sectors. With the important assistance of the venture capital industry, and the passage of the Bayh-Dole Act in 1980, which allowed universities to take out patents on inventions that had been supported by federal tax revenues, they have played an expanding role in the commercial introduction of technologies that were incubated within the university community itself.

American leadership in the biotechnology industry has also been overwhelmingly dependent upon university research, much of it in the medical schools. The key event here was the development of a method for gene splicing (recombinant DNA) by Stanley Cohen of the Stanford Department of Genetics and Herbert Boyer of the University of California, San Francisco in 1973. The technique of genetic engineering has been especially significant in transforming the very nature of the R&D process in pharmaceuticals, although it has potentially important implications for agriculture and food processing as well. An especially interesting aspect of the biotechnology industry has been the prominence of university faculty, not just in research, but in undertaking an entrepreneurial role, typically with considerable financial support from venture capital firms. "[M]any of the leading biotechnology researchers in US universities are also heavily involved with new biotechnology firms, and a good deal of their publishing activity involves collaboration with industrial researchers. University-industry linkages in research, training, and commercialization of new discoveries have been indispensable (and occasionally, controversial) elements in the development of the US biotechnology industry."[27]

American universities look very different when seen from the perspective of schools of engineering and Academic Medical Centers rather than from the perspective of traditional science departments. But that perspective is essential to an understanding of the role that these universities currently play in the life of the American economy – especially as producers of new technological knowledge. This role is sharply delineated in the consolidated budget for R&D expenditures of American academic institutions (see Table 1). Total R&D expenditures in 1996 amounted to $20.8 billion. The physical sciences (primarily chemistry, physics, and astronomy) received only 9.8 per cent of that total. The engineering disciplines received far more than the physical sciences: 16 per cent, or 19.1 per cent if one includes computer science. But the overriding fact is that university R&D budgets are now, and have been for some time, totally dominated by the life sciences, which accounted for 55.2 per cent of the 1996 total. Equally striking in the present context is that the medical sciences accounted for precisely half of that 55.2 per cent, or 27.6 per cent. The high share already attained by the life sciences as early as 1973 largely reflects the rising share of the NIH in the federal R&D budget during the 1950s and 1960s. Between 1950 and 1965 the NIH budget for biomedical research grew by no less than 18 per cent per year in real terms. Medical and engineering R&D expenditures together are now not far from absorbing one half of university budgets (46.7 per cent).[28]

The present dominance of the life sciences in American universities reflects, of course, the expectation of eventual high economic and social returns to research in these fields, and the willingness of the federal government to invest in a field (health-related scientific research) that now has strong public support. Although comparable figures for the university R&D budgets of other OECD countries are not available, a breakdown for six OECD countries (including the US) of "National Expenditures on Academic and Related Research" for the year 1987 is illuminating (Table 2). For that year the life sciences accounted for 48.9 per cent of US national expenditures on academic and related research. The next highest budget, in percentage terms, was for the Federal Republic of Germany (36.7 per cent), followed by France (34.7 per cent), Japan (33.7 per cent), The Netherlands (32.7 per cent), and the UK (30.9 per cent). In the physical sciences, on the other hand, the US was second from the lowest, with a commitment of 15.6 per cent, whereas the average for the rest of the group was 22.2 per cent. It is also important to note the absolute dollar amounts involved in these international comparisons, in addition to the shares of research budgets. US spending on R&D in the life sciences in 1987 far exceeded (by 45 per cent) the sum total for the other five countries.

An examination of these numbers is consistent with the view that the US university system has, once again, responded rapidly to the perception of a new set of economic opportunities. These opportunities have been mainly thrown up by fundamental discoveries in molecular biology, and US universities appear to have responded, far more quickly than universities in other OECD countries, to the

Table 1 Share of academic R&D in a science and engineering field – total, Federal, and nonfederal: 1973, 1980, 1990, and 1996

Fields	Total R&D			
	1973	1980	1990	1996
Total academic R&D	(1992 constant US$ million)			
	8,379	10,227	17,483	20,846
Total of all S&E fields	(per cent)			
	100.0	100.0	100.0	100.0
Engineering	11.6	14.2	16.3	16.0
Aeronautical and astronautical	NA	0.9	1.0	1.0
Chemical engineering	NA	1.0	1.3	1.4
Civil engineering	NA	1.4	1.7	2.0
Electrical engineering	NA	3.0	4.1	3.8
Mechanical engineering	NA	2.3	2.4	2.3
Metallurgical and materials	NA	NA	1.7	1.6
Other engineering	11.6	5.6	4.1	4.0
Physical sciences	11.4	11.2	11.1	9.8
Astronomy	0.8	1.0	1.0	1.2
Chemistry	3.9	4.0	4.0	3.5
Physics	5.8	5.3	5.2	4.3
Other physical sciences	0.8	0.9	0.9	0.8
Environmental sciences	7.3	8.4	6.6	6.4
Atmospheric	NA	1.3	1.1	1.0
Earth sciences	NA	3.1	2.2	2.0
Oceanography	NA	2.9	2.3	2.3
Other environmental sciences	7.3	1.1	1.0	1.2
Mathematical sciences	1.3	1.3	1.4	1.3
Computer sciences	1.2	2.0	3.2	3.1
Life sciences	53.0	53.1	53.6	55.2
Agricultural sciences	9.6	11.1	8.3	8.2
Biological sciences	19.3	17.0	17.6	17.3
Medical sciences	22.4	23.5	25.5	27.6
Other life sciences	1.8	1.5	2.2	2.1
Psychology	2.6	1.8	1.6	1.6
Social sciences	8.0	5.6	4.3	4.8
Economics	1.7	1.5	1.2	1.2
Political science	0.9	0.9	0.7	0.8
Sociology	2.1	1.4	0.8	1.0
Other social sciences	3.3	1.8	1.6	1.8
Other sciences	3.7	2.4	2.1	1.8

Sources: National Science Foundation, Division of Science Resources Studies, Survey of Scientific and Engineering Expenditures at Universities and Colleges; CASPAR Database System (http://caspar.nsf.gov/webcaspar/).

Federal R&D				Nonfederal R&D			
1973	1980	1990	1996	1973	1980	1990	1996
(1992 constant US$ million)							
5,768	6,913	10,345	12,519	2,611	3,314	7,138	8,327
(per cent)							
100.0	100.0	100.0	100.0	100.0	100.0	100.0	100.0
12.0	14.4	15.8	16.0	10.6	13.8	17.0	15.9
NA	1.0	1.3	1.2	NA	0.6	0.5	0.7
NA	1.0	1.1	1.2	NA	1.1	1.6	1.5
NA	1.3	1.2	1.4	NA	1.5	2.5	2.8
NA	3.4	4.5	4.3	NA	2.3	3.5	3.1
NA	2.3	2.5	2.5	NA	2.4	2.3	2.0
NA	NA	1.4	1.4	NA	NA	2.0	1.9
12.0	5.5	3.8	4.0	10.6	6.0	4.5	4.0
13.5	13.5	13.6	11.9	6.7	6.2	7.4	6.8
0.9	1.1	1.2	1.3	0.7	0.7	0.9	1.0
4.4	4.6	4.6	4.1	3.0	2.8	3.1	2.6
7.3	6.8	6.8	5.5	2.4	2.2	2.9	2.5
0.9	1.0	1.1	1.0	0.5	0.6	0.6	0.6
7.9	9.1	7.1	7.2	5.8	6.9	5.8	5.3
NA	1.6	1.4	1.3	NA	0.6	0.6	0.5
NA	3.2	2.1	1.9	NA	2.9	2.3	2.0
NA	3.3	2.7	2.6	NA	2.0	1.7	1.7
7.9	1.0	0.9	1.3	5.8	1.4	1.2	1.1
1.4	1.5	1.7	1.5	0.9	0.9	0.9	0.9
1.3	2.1	3.6	3.7	1.2	1.9	2.6	2.1
51.1	51.0	52.7	53.5	57.3	57.4	54.8	57.8
4.8	5.1	3.7	4.0	20.3	23.8	15.0	14.5
20.1	18.6	19.1	18.6	17.6	13.6	15.3	15.3
24.5	25.8	27.7	28.9	17.8	18.5	22.3	25.7
1.8	1.5	2.2	1.9	1.7	1.5	2.2	2.3
3.0	2.0	1.7	1.8	1.7	1.5	1.3	1.3
6.7	4.4	2.3	3.1	11.0	8.0	7.2	7.4
1.1	1.1	0.6	0.7	2.8	2.4	2.2	2.0
0.5	0.6	0.3	0.5	1.7	1.6	1.4	1.3
2.0	1.4	0.6	0.9	2.3	1.6	1.1	1.2
3.0	1.4	0.9	1.1	4.2	2.5	2.5	2.8
3.1	1.9	1.4	1.2	4.9	3.5	3.0	2.7

Note: NA = not available

Table 2 Breakdown of national expenditures on academic and related research by main field, 1987 (US$ million)[a]

	UK	FRG
Engineering	436 15.6%	505 12.5%
Physical sciences	565 20.2%	1,015 25.1%
Environmental sciences	188 6.7%	183 4.5%
Maths and computing	209 7.5%	156 3.9%
Life sciences	864 30.9%	1,483 36.7%
Social sciences (and psychology)	187 6.7%	210 5.2%
Professional and vocational	161 5.7%	203 5.0%
Arts and humanities	184 6.6%	251 6.2%
Multidisciplinary	6 0.2%	32 0.8%
Total	2,798 100%	4,037 100%

Sources: Irvine, J., Martin, B., and Isard, P., *Investing in the Future: An International Comparison of Government Funding of Academic and Related Research*. Aldershot, Edward Elgar, 1990, p. 219.

Notes:
a　Expenditure data are based on OECD "purchasing power parities" for 1987 calculated in early 1989.
b　This represents an unweighted average for the six countries (i.e., national figures have not been weighted to take into account the differing sizes of countries).

economic potential held out by these discoveries. These transitions are consistent with my view that American universities constitute, among other things, a huge economic enterprise, one that has been powerfully shaped by, and been highly responsive to, economic forces. But the universities are also, by their very success, reshaping the structure and performance of the American economy in ways that we

France	Neths	US	Japan	Average[b]
359	112	1,966	809	
11.2%	11.7%	13.2%	21.6%	14.3%
955	208	2,325	543	
29.7%	21.7%	15.6%	14.5%	21.2%
172	27	859	136	
5.3%	2.8%	5.8%	3.7%	4.8%
175	34	596	88	
5.4%	3.5%	4.0%	2.3%	4.4%
1,116	313	7,285	1,261	
34.7%	32.7%	48.9%	33.7%	36.3%
146	99	754	145	
4.6%	10.4%	5.1%	3.9%	6.0%
67	82	490	369	
2.1%	8.5%	3.3%	9.9%	5.8%
218	83	411	358	
6.8%	8.6%	2.8%	9.6%	6.8%
3	1	217	28	
0.1%	0.1%	1.5%	0.8%	0.6%
3,212	958	14,904	3,736	
100%	100%	100%	100%	100%

do not yet fully appreciate. For example, the success of university research in biomedical R&D has powerfully strengthened the incentives to perform R&D in the private sector. Although it is not widely appreciated, by the 1990s most of the funds for biomedical R&D in the US originated in the private, and not the public, sector. I conclude that American universities have been especially successful as producers of economically useful knowledge. But I also hope that it is now obvious that this is a very big subject, and that my analysis represents only an initial reconnaissance mission in identifying important portions of a vastly larger terrain, not only in the US but in other countries as well. Much more remains to be done.

Chapter 4

Innovators and "mere imitators"

Introduction

In this chapter I would like to explore some connections between innovation and productivity growth. It hardly needs to be added that this was a connection that was of central interest to Schumpeter. After all, it was axiomatic to Schumpeter that capitalism was capable – uniquely capable – of raising the standard of material wellbeing of the great mass of the population. It should be noticed that here too Schumpeter was in agreement with Marx, but only up to a point. For Marx, capitalism's ability to generate growth eventually ran into certain inherent and insurmountable internal contradictions, whereas for Schumpeter capitalism was free of such purely economic flaws. Indeed, Schumpeter confidently asserted that a capitalist economy such as the US, if left to itself, would soon "do away with anything that according to present standards could be called poverty, even in the lowest strata of the population, pathological cases alone excepted." And, of course, Schumpeter was right.[1]

But I have chosen to discuss the connections between innovation and productivity growth not only because it was of interest to a great economist whose memory we honor in these lectures; the subject is also, of course, one of compelling interest throughout the world today. I am tempted to say that, in one sense, Schumpeter may have been too successful in persuading economists of the contribution of innovation to productivity growth. I say this because, at least in the US today, a constant refrain is that we seem to be living in an era of dramatically rapid technological change, and yet these changes appear to be coexisting with an overall rate of productivity improvement that, since the early 1970s, has hovered far below the rates that prevailed in the US in the century or so before 1970. Such discussions involve an almost obligatory reference to Moore's Law, which states that the computing power embedded in a silicon chip can be made to double every 18 months or so. But as often as one hears of Moore's Law, one also hears quoted the pithy observation of Robert Solow that "We see computers everywhere except in the productivity statistics." What, we must ask, is going on? Why do we not observe a higher rate of productivity growth in association with an apparently rapid rate of technological change? That is what I want to discuss in this chapter. Inevitably, the answer to such an unstructured question ("What's going on?") is that a great many things are going on, and I will necessarily have to be very selective in my treatment. But you will not be totally surprised to hear that the analysis will take us, in some important ways, back to Schumpeter.

Connecting technological change with productivity growth

Why is it so difficult to connect new technologies with future productivity growth? A short answer is that it is far from clear, at the outset, what the eventual useful applications of a new technological capability will be. Many, or most, of these potential applications are only teased out gradually over the course of the lifespan of a new technology. This is partly because new technologies are crude and perform poorly at the outset. Their impact on productivity turns very heavily on shaking out numerous uncertainties connected with their initial poor performance.[2] But this is, inevitably, very difficult, as becomes apparent if we take even the briefest glance at what some of the major technologies of the century looked like when they were first being hatched.

In the case of some of these technologies the first and most basic uncertainty was purely technological: would the technology actually work at all? At the very beginning of this century the question was whether heavier-than-air flight was even possible. That question remained unresolved until the Wright brothers actually did it, when they managed to get airborne for just a few brief seconds at Kitty Hawk, South Carolina in December 1903.

No one was certain that nuclear power was possible until an atomic bomb was successfully detonated in New Mexico in the summer of 1945. In fact, some of the world's most distinguished physicists, including the great Lord Rutherford, assured the world in the early 1930s that the very idea of releasing energy from the nucleus of the atom was "hogwash." Nevertheless, during a brief period in that summer of 1945 the most important and closely guarded secret in the world was, quite simply, that the atomic bomb did actually "work" – although only a tiny handful of distinguished physicists understood exactly how.

But the technological uncertainties are only a small part of the story, even though they can sometimes be very dramatic, as in the two cases just cited. From an economic point of view the far more interesting issue is how society will make use of a new technological capability, once that capability has been established. The first central point that needs to be made, then, is that in the history of major new technologies, not only have there been huge uncertainties at the outset concerning their applications, but those uncertainties have persisted as the technology has continued to be improved, even after it has been around for several decades. The camera is, after all, now more than 150 years old, but at the moment it is far from clear how the camera industry is going to be transformed by the advent of digital imaging, which makes possible the electronic storage and transmission of high quality pictures. But, rest assured, it will be transformed.

This sort of uncertainty is what has made it so difficult to connect new technologies with the contributions they might eventually make to productivity improvement. And this is an appropriate point at which to raise a key question: how does one go about measuring the contribution to productivity of a new digital imaging technology that makes it possible to transmit high resolution pictures to anyone with access to a personal computer – whether that person is a distinguished radiologist at some distant medical center or an elderly couple anxious to catch their first glimpse of a brand new grandchild? The issues here are both wide-ranging and subtle. It is one thing to know the price of a PC; it is a very different thing to measure the enlarged flow of services – of output – that a new generation of computers makes possible. This is a key issue in estimating the productivity growth that flows from a new technology.[3]

Thus, to understand the eventual impact of a new technology upon productivity growth, I am suggesting that it is necessary to understand its trajectory of later improvement, and those trajectories are typically in the hands of Schumpeterian "imitators." I personally doubt that, if some of us had seen the Wright brothers' airplane leave the ground on its brief flight back in 1903, we would have left the scene with visions of airplanes crossing the Atlantic Ocean in six hours or so carrying 350 people watching movies in at least some reasonable degree of comfort. (In my own experience, often the only genuine source of discomfort is the quality of the onboard movie!) In fact, almost seventy years elapsed between the Wright brothers and the introduction of the 747. It even took a full third of a century before a much more modest set of improvements in airplane design, structure, and components were incorporated in the DC-3 (1936), the introduction of which marked the beginning of commercial aviation.[4]

This vision of major innovations as made up of numerous incremental improvements, extending out over lengthy periods of time, and the cumulative importance of which is of decisive economic significance, is very different from the one offered by Schumpeter. Now, in my view, Schumpeter was one of the very greatest economists of the twentieth century, and we owe to him our deeper awareness of how central the process of innovation is to productivity improvement and therefore to economic growth. But Schumpeter, I believe, attached excessive importance to a single event: the first introduction of an innovation into the market place, and the numerous difficulties encountered by the entrepreneur in achieving that introduction. From that point on, he proceeded to analyze what he called "the process of creative destruction," a form of competition vastly different, as he correctly emphasized, from the traditional textbook analysis of price competition that prevailed in his own day, involving a large number of small competitors producing a homogeneous, or slightly heterogeneous, commodity.[5]

I have enormous respect for the illuminating power of Schumpeter's insight into the functioning of the capitalist market place. He helped immeasurably in explaining how the organization of economic life is transformed by technological change. But, in one important respect, he made the process appear to be a good deal simpler than in fact it is. And this oversimplification, together with Schumpeter's vast influence, may have had at least something to do with the recent widespread disappointment that the impact of major new technologies has not yet shown up more conspicuously in measures of productivity improvement. For Schumpeter paid far less attention to technological change after that first introduction to the market place had been accomplished. He appreciated that entrepreneurs are compelled to make financial decisions of great consequence under circumstances of very limited information. But in his world the successful completion of an innovation resolves the major uncertainties that had previously existed. Once his charismatic entrepreneurs have done their essential work, the stage is then set for imitators whose activities, although requiring no high levels of talent, are nevertheless responsible for the subsequent diffusion of the new technology.

Schumpeter was fond of speaking of "mere imitators," because in his view all they needed to do is to follow in the footsteps of the entrepreneurs who have led the way, and whose earlier activities have resolved all the big uncertainties. My own view is that, on the contrary, these so-called "mere imitators" may be far more than imitators.[6] In fact, they have commonly been the essential carriers of an improvement process that decisively shapes the eventual contribution of new technologies to productivity improvement. To revert to the airplane: if technological change in aircraft had ended with the Wright brothers, however remarkable their first achievement truly was, the airplane would still be a flimsy contraption – a biplane made of wood and cloth, held together by sealing wax and baling wire, with a capability of flying the length of a couple of football fields, and rising to just a few feet off the ground. In fact, on the very first flight at Kitty Hawk, on December 17, 1903, the plane flew a distance of just 120 feet. And when the Army Signal Corps took its courage in its hands and finally decided to order its first airplane five years later (1908), the crucial contractual specification – crucial because it was not obvious at the time that it would be fulfilled – was that the aircraft had to attain a speed of 40 miles per hour!

Clearly, Schumpeter's celebration of the dynamic role of the entrepreneur provides little space for the activities of those who followed in the entrepreneur's footsteps. In fact, the very analogy of "following in the footsteps" is an ill-chosen one with respect to major innovations. For it is precisely the subsequent improvement process that has converted primitive, useless contraptions, such as the airplane of 1903 vintage, to high performance technologies of major economic significance.

Schumpeter would not, of course, have denied the economic importance of the post-innovation improvement process. Nor was he unaware that new technologies that are built upon the scaffolding of earlier technologies will often come to qualify as major innovations in their own right. But these matters simply held little interest for him. His "vision" (see Chapter 1 of this volume) and his sociology led him to insist upon the sharp disjunction between invention and innovation, on the one hand, and between innovation and imitation, on the other. In establishing the meaning that he attached to the term "innovation," he warned his readers:

> It should be noticed at once that the concept is not synonymous with "invention." Whatever the latter term may mean, it has but a distant relation to ours. . . . The making of the invention and the carrying out of the corresponding innovation are, economically and sociologically, two entirely different things.[7]

This proclaimed disinterest in inventive activity also helps to account for Schumpeter's lack of interest in the post-innovation technological improvement process.

Technological complementarities

There is an additional level of complexity that appears, historically, to have been crucially important, at least occasionally, in shaping the eventual consequences of new technologies. Sometimes it will turn out that two previously unrelated technologies can be combined in a way that will powerfully strengthen the effectiveness of one of them, or that, *in combination*, the two will provide a new platform that opens up a whole realm of new commercial possibilities. In other words, there is a relationship of complementarity, in that an improvement in one technology will enhance the performance of, and presumably increase the demand for, the other.

Consider the electronic digital computer which, once it became available in September 1945, had only very limited uses for a number of years. In fact, surprising as it may seem in retrospect, IBM, whose name was later to become virtually synonymous with computers, waited several years before it decided to enter the computer market. The main reason why the computer appeared to have such poor prospects in the years immediately after World War II was that it was still dependent for its operation on the vacuum tube. The great revolution in computer technology – perhaps I should say the first great revolution in computer technology since there have been several – came when the integrated circuit, containing many transistors, was incorporated into the computer, as a substitute for the vacuum tube and the single transistor, in the 1960s.[8] This represented a striking synergy between two separate and apparently unrelated technologies that opened entirely new realms of possibilities.

An equally striking relationship of unexpected complementarities has occurred with respect to fiber optics and the laser. The laser, in combination with fiber optics, has been transforming the worldwide telecommunication systems, including, of course, data transmission and video transmission as well as the traditional functions of the telephone. With respect to the telephone, the best transatlantic telephone cables in 1966 could carry simultaneously only 138 conversations between Europe and North America. The first fiber optic cable, installed in 1988, can carry 40,000, and the fiber optic cables installed in the 1990s can carry more.[9] And yet it was reported that the patent lawyers at Bell Labs were initially unwilling even to apply for a patent on the laser, on the grounds that optical technologies had no possible relevance to the telephone industry. In the words of Charles Townes, who subsequently won a Nobel prize for his research on the laser, "Bell's patent department at first refused to patent our amplifier or oscillator for optical frequencies because, it was explained, optical waves had never been of any importance to communications and hence the invention had little bearing on Bell System interests."[10]

It would be easy to congratulate ourselves on how much smarter and wiser we are than the legal staff in Bell's patent department who were unable to foresee what is so perfectly obvious to us, i.e., the enormous potential value of fiber optics to the telephone industry. And of course almost everyone (in America at least) welcomes the opportunity to feel superior to lawyers. But that would be a mistaken conceit. The reason is that the possibility of combining two new technological capabilities to achieve a purpose that had no apparent connection with either was anything but obvious. The fact is that, although optical frequency laser devices were being operated as early as 1960,[11] it took many years of research and experimentation before a full appreciation of the attractive characteristics of fiber optics technology was attained. The lack of electromagnetic interference, the conservation of heat and electricity, and the enormous expansion in bandwidth that fiber optics provides are all features whose utility became apparent only years later with the decision of new long-distance firms such as MCI (Microwave Communications Inc.) and Sprint to invest in the new technology. This growing commitment of resources to investment in fiber optic technology, it should be noted, was greatly strengthened by the increasingly competitive market structure in telecommunications following the divestiture of AT&T in 1984.

The revolution that is currently underway in telecommunications has, at its center, a combination of the separate capabilities of optical fibers and laser beams. Neither of these two technologies had identifiable uses when they first emerged. The earliest use of fiber optics was in the second half of the 1950s, when it was introduced into medical diagnostics in the form of a flexible endoscope that was used to examine the gastrointestinal tract. The expansion of applications of optical fibers owed a great deal to ongoing improvements in the quality of glass, improvements in which the Corning Glass firm played a crucial role.[12] The possibility of anticipating, in the early stages, how the two technologies might later be used in combination was surely negligible, but the key link was that, in addition to much greater bandwidth, the transmission of light over high quality optical fibers could now be achieved with little attenuation of signals, even over long distances.

Thus, in the course of technological development in advanced industrial societies, it has occasionally happened that a particular technology emerged that provided strong opportunities for complementarity with other technologies. The number of technologies that have done this has not been very great: the steam engine, machine tools, electricity (generators and motors), transistors, computers. These technologies have each provided a platform on which numerous complementary technologies have been built, and it is my belief that lasers are already well on the way to joining this small, exclusive club. These general purpose technologies (GPTs), as they have come to be called, are now beginning to receive considerable attention from economists. The fact that they have the common characteristic of providing opportunities for other technologies to be built upon them suggests that they may play a critical role in productivity growth.

The laser

Consider the laser, then, as a prime candidate for the status of a GPT. I have emphasized so far the role it has come to play in the spectacular improvements in information and telecommunications technologies. But, at the same time, it has provided a platform for a bewildering array of innovations in a large number of sectors of economic life. Although the underlying technology and its scientific principles are of course common to all its applications, the economic and social contexts, in many cases, appear to be quite unrelated. Again, the difficulties here were not fundamentally technological, although a considerable amount of time had to be spent in coming to appreciate some of the specific characteristics of the technology before it was possible to make links to various categories of uses. Rather, the difficulties lay in linking these performance characteristics into a variety of contexts where they could provide a platform for innovative activity in both products and services.

I suspect that the laser is still in the early stages of its trajectory of growth as a GPT, but it has already proven its role as a source of "innovational complementarities." That is to say, a main feature of a GPT is that it makes possible an increase in the productivity of R&D in a number of "downstream" sectors of the economy. More specifically, as the GPT advances, it enlarges the range of opportunities for downstream applications, and the awareness of such possibilities, in turn, feeds back upon the incentive to perform R&D in the GPT sector as well as downstream. Consequently, there is a dynamic interaction between research at the GPT level and in the applications sectors. Thus, the possibilities for pervasive use of a GPT become a basis for widespread improvements in productivity.[13]

These innovational complementarities have already given rise to a range of new technologies that are, in various ways, "plugged into" the laser. Undoubtedly the most important application so far has been the one already mentioned: its current, ongoing role in the transformation of telecommunications. Consider further, however, the enormous range of activities over which the laser is currently exercising some impact:

1   The laser has become a primary instrument of scientific and engineering research due to its ability to perform measurements with a degree of precision previously impossible, but also to generate and thus to observe physical transformations that were not previously observable. "Measurements have been and are being made that simply could not be made in any other fashion. Chemistry, biology and physics laboratories use many types of lasers to probe, measure and modify the fundamental properties of matter." In engineering laboratories, "laser beams are projected into huge wind tunnels to measure local flow velocity and turbulence," and thus to assist in aircraft design.[14] The Nobel prize in physics in 1997 was awarded for research that had involved extensive use of lasers.

2   In addition to their role in medical research, lasers have become the instrument of choice in a range of surgical procedures. These include a wide variety of extraordinarily delicate procedures upon the eye, such as the repair of detached retinas and reshaping the cornea in order to correct near-sightedness. My ophthalmology clinic in Palo Alto, to which I go periodically for checkups, now has a separate section called the "Laser Center." In gynecological surgery, lasers now provide a simpler and less painful method for removal of certain tumors.[15] Lasers are presently being tested for the treatment of enlarged prostate glands. An impressive index of the impact of the laser in medicine is that there are now four journals, established since 1980, that are devoted *exclusively* to the application of lasers in medicine.[16]

3   The laser has become a multipurpose tool in industry. In textiles it is used to cut cloth to desired shapes, and it is employed for similar uses across many metallurgical sectors, as well as for cutting complex patterns in such materials as plywood, glass, and plastics. Gillette razor blades are now welded by laser. In food processing, lasers are being used, so far only experimentally, to identify contaminated meat. Surely we all wish this last undertaking "Godspeed!"

4   The most successful computer printers are based upon laser technology (HP laserjet printer). Lasers are also widely used in typesetting, newspaper plate making, and the printing industry more generally.

5   Lasers are now the basic technology employed inside the bar code scanners at checkout counters in supermarkets, as well as in libraries, in inventory control technologies, and in security devices in department stores.

6   Lasers are now the technology of choice for the high quality reproduction of music in compact disks.

7   The military applications of the laser are fast multiplying. They are being used as triggers for nuclear bombs, and also for directing so-called "smart bombs" and missiles to their targets. Lasers have also been widely touted as the key to anti-missile devices, although there continues to be much disagreement on the potential effectiveness of this application. The Lawrence Livermore weapons laboratory, no doubt out of a concern with protecting its huge budget by developing civilian applications for their lasers, recently reported that it had created a

portable laser that can obliterate graffiti from walls at lightning speed.[17]

8   Finally, to draw from a recent miscellany: (a) in October 1997 advertisements began to appear in US newspapers offering "skin resurfacing" by use of lasers, a procedure, as the ads warned, that should be performed only by plastic surgeons (and not, presumably, by dermatologists); (b) lasers are fast becoming the instrument of choice for the removal of unwanted body hair: cosmetic laser "spas" have made their appearance all over the US, and elsewhere, in the last couple of years, replacing the older electrolysis methods, even though they are substantially more expensive (in this case it is the dermatologists who warn that the procedure should only be performed under "proper" medical supervision); and (c) applications in dentistry have already received the FDA's "good housekeeping" seal of approval.

With respect to this extraordinary diversity of applications, let me suggest a thought experiment. Think back to the early 1960s, after laser action had already been achieved, and even assume, if you wish, that the characteristics of the laser were already well understood – which, it is important to remember, they were not. Which of the eventual uses of the laser, just enumerated, do you think you would have forecast? And notice that I have not even mentioned the much more complicated case of telecommunications, where the use of the laser required the simultaneous development of another truly major complementary invention: fiber optics. I would like to be the first to insist that I would not have forecast any of the applications that I have just mentioned.

The history of the laser over the past forty years or so prompts the serious reflection that the most important of all inventive activities may be the identification of new uses for technological capabilities that have already been invented. This is, in fact, my main reservation concerning the Schumpeterian conceptualization of the process of innovation: it focused attention excessively upon the earliest stages of a much more complex and elongated process, thus leading to the comparative neglect of later activities that deserve far more attention. The recent growth of interest in GPTs is doubly welcome because it pays particular attention to the dynamics of technological change in the period that Schumpeter left to "mere imitators."

What do "imitators" do?

An important inference that I would like to draw from these observations concerning lasers is that the widespread diffusion and, therefore, the productivity impact of GPTs, depends upon the success of subsequent research directed toward specific applications. The experience with lasers is useful to consider because it dramatizes the very wide range of apparently unrelated activities where a new technological capability may eventually find applications. At the same time, it is difficult in the extreme to define a search strategy or a new system of incentives that will lead in a faster, more socially efficient manner than the capitalist market place, to the complementary innovations through which GPTs deliver their productivity benefits. The one totally unambiguous lesson of history is that the process takes a long time.

If one looks at the early experience of electricity for some guidance, as several economists have done, it appears that it took about forty years (from the 1880s to the 1920s) before the commercial availability of electricity had been translated into measurable productivity improvement in American factories.[18] But the history of electricity is not a story in which a new technology became available in the 1880s and then simply diffused very slowly for forty years or so. In fact, those years were years of intense further inventive activity in which the essential components of a much larger technological system were created. This system came to include the steam turbine, insulators, transformers, and other technologies that were essential to transmission, and the electric motor which was, of course, the key complementary invention for purposes of many later household as well as industrial applications. The meter for measuring electricity consumption was far from the least important addition to the system for the delivery of electricity. Until the availability of a reliable meter, it was a common practice to charge the customer by the number of electrical fixtures installed rather than by the amount of electricity actually consumed!

Numerous further applications awaited not only the slow, cumulative reductions in the cost of generation and transmission, but also further inventive activity that was necessary in numerous applications sectors, such as metallurgy, which is currently the largest industrial user of electricity.

Although the electric arc furnace was developed in the late nineteenth century, its use in the steel industry was limited to a small number of specialty steels for many years. It was only after World War II, by which time substantial further reductions in the cost of electricity had been achieved, that the electric furnace came to play a major role in the manufacture of steel.

As recently as the early 1960s, the use of the electric furnace was still confined to sophisticated products such as alloys and stainless steels, and "mini-mills" accounted for less than 9 per cent of US raw steel production in 1961. By 1970 this share had grown to over 15 per cent. Since that year, essentially all new capacity installed in the American steel industry has consisted of mini-mills, and by 1999 the mini-mill's share of domestic US steel production was approaching 50 per cent.[19]

Thus, it would be fair to say that it took almost one hundred years before electricity achieved its present dominant status in the manufacture of steel. But the story is not, of course, one of "mere imitators"; rather, it is one of major improvements and cost reductions in the generation of electricity, and also of advances on the part of the application sectors – in this case in the mini-mill technology – that made possible the electrification of the steel industry.

A similar story of reliance upon electricity could be told with respect to aluminum, an extremely versatile metal that became the second most important primary metal in the American economy in the course of the twentieth century. Although the origins of the electrolytic process that made aluminum commercially feasible go back to the 1880s, it experienced an explosive growth only in the second half of the twentieth century, especially in the transportation sector. The processing of aluminum has remained not only energy-intensive but, more specifically, highly electricity-intensive, as remains even more true of its recycling.

Since there has been a great deal of impatience and frustration with low rates of productivity growth, knowledge of the slow growth of productivity from electricity may simply confirm the feelings of distress. Many of the economic benefits of electricity, a nineteenth-century innovation, made themselves felt in four decades or so. Many of the major benefits of electricity in metallurgy, however, took a great deal longer, which is to say three-quarters of a century and even more. But, looked at differently, the history of technology may be a source of some optimism. After all, the computer, surely one of the greatest of all GPTs, has already been around for several decades, if one dates it from the primitive device that became available in 1945. It may therefore be reasonable to speculate that a heightened flow of productivity benefits deriving from the computer will soon, or at least eventually, become available. We have simply failed to anticipate the difficulties of developing the complementary technologies, as the concept of GPTs now usefully reminds us. Let me make three observations on this issue.

1   Although the computer has indeed been around for more than fifty years, if we date it from the ENIAC, its original crudeness and unreliability rendered it quite unsuitable for widespread applications. The commercial exploitation of the computer had to await a series of further improvements involving, not only the use of the transistor beginning in the late 1950s but also the far more important integrated circuit of the 1960s, the spinning off and creation of a separate software sector in the late 1960s, the invention of the microprocessor (essentially an extraordinary extension of the integrated circuit) at the beginning of the 1970s, and the invention and widespread diffusion of the personal computer in the 1980s, along with a partial displacement of the mainframe computer. In the 1990s, in one of the most remarkable of all transformations in the history of technology, a device that had been invented for the purpose of computing was converted into an amazingly effective device for communicating. Indeed, the very term "computer" has become something of an anachronism, like the second "T" that is still retained in the name "AT&T."[20]

The Internet and the World Wide Web, which exploited the capability of the new personal computers, have their own most unlikely origins in the Pentagon's search for a communications system that would be totally decentralized and would therefore reduce the nation's vulnerability to a nuclear attack. But the overriding point for my present purposes is that, in the case of the computer, the GPT itself has gone through quite fundamental changes of its own, so that the platform upon which the applications sectors can build has itself been fundamentally transformed. Today's computer platform is worlds away from IBM's System/360 that so dominated the 1960s. The Internet may, in fact, be thought of as another complementary technology that was made possible by the gigantic, expanded capacities of today's computers. Thus, it is not unreasonable to expect greater productivity benefits from the computer than we were entitled to expect twenty or twenty-five years ago from a primitive ancestor of the present-day computer.

2   But why isn't more productivity improvement already apparent? There are, to begin with, serious measurement problems in dealing with productivity growth.[21] In general, present measurement conventions capture improvements in productivity that take the form of simple cost reductions much better than they capture improvements in performance or quality, or the availability of products that are "fine-tuned" so as to be better suited to the needs of specific classes of customers. Furthermore, established practices of the Bureau of Labor Statistics systematically fail to capture the full impact of new products. New products are introduced into measures of cost and output with a considerable time lag. For example, microwave ovens sold for around $1,500 when they were first put on the market, but they entered into BLS measurements only much later when they sold for as little as $200. Similarly, the video cassette recorder (VCR) was introduced into the Consumer Price Index in 1987, a full decade after it had begun selling in considerable volume.

But there have been even more extreme omissions. Cellular telephones were first offered for sale in 1983. When AT&T was being divested in 1984, it issued a prediction, based on a study by a consulting firm, that in the year 1999 US subscription levels for cellular phones might stand at around 1 million. In fact, at the end of 1996, that figure was already about 42 million,[22] and, in April 1999, the Cellular Telecommunications Industry Association reported that subscriptions stood at over 69 million. Cellular phone adoptions have been growing at an annual rate of between 25 and 35 per cent. Of course, huge price reductions have been an essential part of the story, and their prospective impact on future demand seems to have been grossly underestimated. Whereas cellular phones sold for about $3,000 in 1983, they were readily available in 1997 at well under $200.[23] Subscribers in 1997 were spending about $26 billion a year on cellular service, an amount equal to about one-third of all long-distance telephone revenues, and the number of cellular phones then in use was equal to one-third of all regular telephones. It seems obvious that this new technology has been a valuable and productive instrument for at least some of its users. Yet the BLS did not include cellular phones in constructing its Consumer Price Index until 1998.

Thus, the official BLS figures fail to capture the price declines, sometimes large, that often occur in the early stages of the product cycle. But, perhaps even more important, the prevailing practice is to measure the price of goods without taking adequate account of the increasing volume of services that may be flowing from such goods. In a nutshell, the practice is to measure the price of light bulbs rather than the price of light,[24] or the purchase price of truck tires rather than the cost per mile traveled.

Nevertheless, having said this, the scale of the decline in productivity growth appears to have been far greater than can reasonably be attributed to measurement problems. If measurement problems are invoked to account for the apparent slowdown in US productivity growth over the past thirty years, it would be necessary to argue that the size of the measurement bias had increased over that period of time, because the kinds of biases that I have referred to have certainly been around for many years. I am not aware, however, of any demonstration that such biases have in fact grown. One relevant observation, though, and this will lead to my third point, is that measured improvement in labor productivity in US manufacturing moved closer to its long-term, pre-1970 growth rate during the 1990s. Alternatively put, the slow rate of measured productivity growth in the overall US economy in the 1990s was heavily weighted by the slow productivity growth of the service sector.

3 The economy to which computers are now being applied is overwhelmingly a service economy and not a manufacturing economy, and the application of computer capability to such an economy is far more complex than the application of, say, electricity was to the factory. This is so quite apart from the much greater inherent complexity of the interface between the computer and the human agent as compared to the complexity of the interface between electricity and the human agent.

Consider the following two facts:

(a) Well over 70 per cent of the American labor force today is engaged in the service sectors: transportation, communications, finance, insurance, real estate, wholesale and retail trade, health and education, business and personal services, tourism, and government. (Moreover, although it has not been widely noticed, fully 30 per cent of American export earnings are now derived from the provision of services, reflecting a sharp increase in recent years.) By comparison with the more than 70 per cent of the labor force in services, less than 17 per cent are now engaged in manufacturing. Thus, the output of the US economy is now the result of activities of a kind where productivity improvements are more difficult to measure, especially when, as in health care, changes are primarily qualitative in nature.

(b) Computer and information technologies are, overwhelmingly, purchased by these service sectors. Thus, future improvements in productivity will necessarily have to come from a very large number of successful applications of these technologies to the service sectors.

Unfortunately, measurement problems come to haunt us far more in the service sectors than in manufacturing. The difficulties here are quite fundamental in nature: at bottom, it is often impossible to arrive at a satisfactory measure of productivity in services because there exists no clear agreement on what constitutes output. That is to say, the difficulty is really deeper than what is ordinarily meant by reference to "measurement problems."

The question then is this: what is it that really constitutes the "output" of the service sectors? What, for example, is the output of the health care delivery sector which will soon absorb 15 per cent of US GDP? Clearly, much of the technological change in medical care takes the form of unmeasured quality improvement. What is the output of the police force, or the fire department, or the entire government sector, for that matter? And how – dare I ask – is one to measure the output of a college professor? In health care, we know that new surgical procedures, such as laparoscopy, are sharply reducing the length of hospital stays, and new pharmaceutical products, such as Tagamet, have eliminated trips to the hospital altogether. Other new imaging technologies, such as the CT scanner and MRI, have led to earlier diagnosis of many life-threatening conditions, resulting in earlier interventions and improved survival prospects. Nevertheless, measures of service sector productivity growth are, quite simply, dismal, and it is the heavy weight attaching to service sector performance that dominates the low level of measured productivity growth for the US economy as a whole. The growth in the size of the service sector, however, is a long-term trend that extends backward in time for over a century. By itself, there-fore, a long-term trend of service sector growth that is not rapidly accelerating cannot explain more than a small percentage of the measured productivity slowdown of the aggregate economy over the past thirty years.

If it is any source of satisfaction – and of course it should be – a large part of this unmeasured productivity improvement must surely be taking the form of "consumer surplus." That is, the competitive process in a high-tech world is driving down the prices of many goods (especially consumer durable goods) and services, so that consumers are now able to acquire them for a good deal less than they would otherwise have been prepared to pay. This would obviously include a wide range of electronics products, most obviously PCs, VCRs, microwave ovens, etc., but also improvements in "old-fashioned" technologies such as electric lighting. People who would be willing to pay a couple of thousand dollars for a cellular phone, if they had to, can now buy one for fully an order of magnitude less. The widespread ownership of such phones is surely evidence that they represent a large consumer surplus.

To be sure, utilization of some of the new or improved technologies that I have referred to should also have exercised some discernable impact on measured final output, in addition to raising the size of the consumer surplus. Reduced length of hospital stays and faster recovery times from surgery may translate into earlier return to productive employment. Microwave ovens, cellular phones, and automatic teller machines (ATMs) may reduce the time spent in performing routine household and related chores, and some of the time thus saved may be allocated to "productive" activities rather than to increased leisure. I wish only to assert that *some portion* of the utilization of such new technologies constitutes a genuine improvement in consumer welfare, but that another unspecified portion must already be captured by conventional measures of output.

Future prospects

I have been expressing the view that we may be experiencing a good deal more productivity improvement than has been captured by the official measures. However, the important questions are: what are the prospects for future improvements, and what can be said, on the basis of recent history, about the obstacles?

The IT industries (defined broadly to include not only computer-based technologies but telecommunications as well) will certainly be dominated by the continued exploitation of the computer and, I suspect, the laser as well. When we address the question of the innovational complementarities that will be built upon these platforms, it is important to understand that the problems for which solutions need to be found are not simply of a hardware nature. Rather, they also include issues of the internal organization and operation of the firm, of procurement from potential suppliers on the one hand, and advertising and selling to customers on the other. The information technologies, and in particular the Internet and the World Wide Web, have yet to identify fully the roles that they can play in improving the efficiency of the ordinary, prosaic, day-to-day activities of the firm: production scheduling, taking orders from outside buyers, making purchases from outside suppliers, enhancing customer support systems, computing employee benefits, processing expense accounts, etc. Computer-based technologies surely hold out the eventual prospect of the automation of the entire range of corporate transactions in all sectors of the economy.

Let me return again, in closing, to the service sectors that now dominate the economic lives, not just of Americans, but of all the OECD member countries.[25] Consider again medical care, one of the largest of the service sectors. The computer has already had a massive impact on medical care. This can be readily confirmed by just a brisk walk through the intensive care unit of any major teaching hospital. Computers are everywhere, monitoring the patient's cardiovascular status, controlling ventilators that perform respiratory functions when needed, administering drugs, providing instant access to laboratory test results, etc. CT scanners and MRI technology could not function without computers. Moreover, the computer's capacity to store, retrieve, and manipulate huge masses of data has revolutionized biomedical research. But the computer has also been a dismal failure, at least so far, in the attempt to introduce much-needed reforms in Medicare, the country's largest health insurance program. The problems that have been encountered are symptomatic of some of the difficulties in generating productivity improvements from the use of highly sophisticated technologies in service activities. The difficulties are also revealing of a continuing naïveté in invoking the use of powerful technologies in the search for solutions to complex social problems.

In 1994 the American federal government, with great fanfare, hired

General Telephone and Electronics as the main contractor to introduce a computer system that would speed the payment of claims, improve customer service, and combat the rampant fraud within the Medicare system. (A recent audit had shown that Medicare had overpaid health care providers by no less than $23 billion in 1996.) That project was eventually admitted to have been a complete failure. The headline in the September 16, 1997 issue of the *New York Times* read: "Modernization effort for Medicare computer system grinds to halt, thwarted by complexity." Complexity is indeed the key word. The problem was surely not insufficient computing capability, but rather the awesome difficulties in defining the multiple goals that the computer system needed to pursue in the context of the Medicare payment system. The problem was to design a computer program that would incorporate the incredible complexity of categories, exceptions, exemptions, qualifications, restrictions, additions, and contingencies that make up the Medicare payment system. That goal proved, after a couple of years of intense effort, to be unattainable. The Medicare financial system requires considerable reorganization and simplification before it can be successfully computerized. Additionally, of course, the nature and the multiplicity of the social and economic goals that are incorporated in the Medicare program, as well as the politics of introducing changes, may seriously limit the possibilities for extensive simplification.

In citing the difficulties of applying today's information technology to the complexities of the Medicare system I have, admittedly, called attention to an extreme case, but also to an urgent one. Medicare payment benefits are expected to amount to $300 billion in the year 2003. But the general point is that the achievement of productivity gains from major new technological systems requires further, complementary inventive activity of an entirely different nature from those that went into the development and improvement of the hardware. Such inventive activity must be achieved by the eventual users of the new IT, and not by the engineers and scientists whose R&D activities had developed that technology in the first place. Dealing with the financial dimensions of the medical care sector will require innovational initiatives very different from those that led to the endoscope or the CT scanner.

My conclusion, then, is that past history and current experience indicate that a major bottleneck in extracting the benefits from new technologies lies at the applications level, where questions of organization, incentives, patterns of work specialization, and the extremely diverse needs of eventual users, especially in the service sectors, become critical. I would also remind you that Schumpeter himself emphasized that he by no means restricted his definition of "innovation" to hardware, although he remained quite insistent upon maintaining the distinction between innovators and imitators.[26]

What I have said should be taken as a plea to pay more attention to the extremely disorderly process that follows upon the first introduction into the market of a technological innovation. This should include not only the critically important subsequent improvement process, but also the innumerable and subtle ways in which technology is sorted, matched, and modified to suit the huge diversity of ultimate user needs – even including the diversity of needs on the part of the large elderly population whose medical care is now financed by the Medicare system. Americans, especially, have been much too preoccupied with generating new technologies, and far too little concerned with the conditions that need to be fulfilled to achieve an efficient utilization of these technologies. Schumpeter's dismissal of the economic importance of "mere imitators" had the unfortunate consequence of reinforcing the underestimation of the range of creative skills that are required to achieve an efficient use of increasingly sophisticated technologies. I believe that this is what underlies a large part of the failure of computers to show up, as Robert Solow has lamented, in the productivity statistics. But while one side of this coin is that it is taking what seems to be an inordinately long time to extract the benefits, the other, brighter side is that these benefits may still lie before us.

Chapter 5

Chemical engineering as a general purpose technology

Author's note

I have decided to include a shortened version of a recent paper on chemical engineering in this volume because it is, I believe, very much in the Schumpeterian spirit. It was written while I was preparing the Schumpeter lectures but, more importantly, it was influenced by my past reading of Schumpeter. If, indeed, Schumpeter regarded technological change as endogenous, as I have argued, then surely that endogeneity must include the growing body of technological knowledge that provided the intellectual basis for the design and construction of new technologies.

While engaged in research on innovation in the chemical sector, it became apparent to me that the success of innovation in that sector depended heavily upon the discipline of chemical engineering. The manufacture of chemical products requires the ability to design and to operate processing plants that can produce such products efficiently. More specifically, economies of scale are a major force in chemical processing plants, and the design of such plants depends crucially upon the ability to convert information derived (or inferred) from smaller scale plants – so-called "pilot plants" – to the optimal proportions of a much larger plant, in order to take advantage of economies of scale. This is precisely the role of chemical engineering.

The discipline of chemical engineering, then, can be regarded as a body of knowledge that has come to play a critical role in the twentieth century in providing the intellectual basis for technological innovations of truly massive importance. These innovations include the refining of petroleum after World War I, which was so central to the diffusion of the automobile, and supplying the intermediate inputs upon which the petrochemical industry of the post World War II period was to be built (plastics, synthetic fibers, synthetic rubber, etc.).

In the first half of the 1990s economists were beginning to explore the notion that some technological innovations were of special significance because they provided the building blocks upon which numerous other innovations were eventually constructed. That is, some technologies can be regarded as general purpose technologies (GPTs) because they provided technological capabilities that could be utilized in a large number of "application sectors." Steam engines, machine tools, electricity, transistors, and computers all fall into this category.

This way of thinking seemed eminently sensible and especially illuminating to someone who has long had a special interest in the history of technologies, and who had in fact written a paper many years ago that explored the relationship between the introduction of a new class of machines – machine tools – and the wide range of their subsequent applications.[1]

But if it is appropriate to think of "pieces of hardware" as constituting GPTs, surely it was equally if not even more appropriate to think of the underlying body of knowledge as having a general purpose nature. That is, one should not think of the engine lathe or the milling machine as the GPT; rather, the real GPT is the knowledge, the mechanical engineering principles, that were incorporated in the lathe or milling machine. In that case, the study of technological change needs to devote far greater attention to the emergence and diffusion of engineering disciplines as the true GPTs, of which specific technologies are merely concrete embodiments.

This was the sequence of reasoning that gave rise to this chapter. But it also became apparent, as we see in the opening pages, that this mode of thinking may also be valuable to the now highly influential New Growth Theory, which reasserts, and formalizes, the endogeneity of technological change.

Introduction

The immediate aim of this chapter is to examine the discipline of chemical engineering as a general purpose technology (GPT), and to look at the relationship between this particular GPT and the rise of its application sectors – primarily petroleum and petrochemicals.

In this context, the chapter explores the notion that it is useful to conceive of a set of ideas as constituting a GPT.[2]

But the chapter is also motivated by another interest. There is widespread agreement that technological change is, at bottom, some kind of learning process. However, the big question is exactly how that learning takes place – specifically, how does society acquire the new knowledge and capabilities that constitute technological change? Economic theorists and economic historians would both agree that growth of knowledge needs to be examined, at least as a starting point, as the outcome of purposive investments by economic agents.

In the New Growth Theory,[3] the entire learning process, and the conditions on which its success and development depend, are represented by inserting two variables into its equations: (a) investment in R&D, and (b) investment in tangible capital (together with some observations about increasing returns and learning by doing). The actual "progress of technology" remains an unopened black box, but the central point is that a new blueprint today spills over to lower the cost of future blueprints. There is, in other words, an intertemporal externality.

The story that will be told here goes a certain distance toward analyzing the contents of that black box in the specific context of chemical engineering. No claim is made that the entire process of learning – of technical progress – has been rendered endogenous, but it is hoped that the questions of explanation have been posed at a deeper level. And it is argued further that, even when one accepts the abstractions of the New Growth Theory and the centrality of the variables on which it focuses, effective policy formulation still requires knowing how to implement that abstract knowledge under practical conditions. Alternatively put, without the presence of the conditions that are examined here, the actual effects of the variables identified in the New Growth Theory remain somewhat uncertain. Perhaps more fully endogenizing the growth of knowledge, upon which technological change depends, calls for a joint enterprise involving theorists, historians, and engineers.

According to the New Growth Theory, all inventive activity reduces the cost of future inventive activity in the same way. What the evidence introduced here really seems to suggest, however, is that a particular type of innovation – in this case the creation of a new disciplinary framework – actually determines the relevant parameters of the degree of intertemporal spillover. Without the formulation of the idea of unit operations, so central as we will see to chemical engineering, a tremendous amount of technological knowledge could not have "spilled over" into the future. Rather, that knowledge would simply have been used in the creation of an idiosyncratic and singular product or process. However, with the development of the concept of unit operations and the codification of such knowledge in textbooks, a given amount of inventive effort led to a potentially larger spillover to future inventors. Thus, the concept of unit operations created an intertemporal spillover that reduced the cost of future inventive activity. In this sense, there is a strong mutual influence between the endogeneity of the New Growth Theory and the existence of the phenomenon of general purpose technologies.

This is the larger context of the present focus on the growth of one particular engineering discipline, chemical engineering. The reasoning is straightforward. If one is interested in how technological learning accumulates, one needs to look carefully at the engineering professions. Most of these professions – such as chemical, electrical, and aeronautical engineering and metallurgy – are relatively new disciplines, none of them much more than a hundred years old. These disciplines came into existence in response to the emergence of new industries, going back to the so-called "Second Industrial Revolution" of the late nineteenth century. And the engineering discipline that is now called "computer science" is, of course, of much more recent vintage.

The engineering disciplines need to be thought of as the repositories of technological knowledge, and their practitioners as the primary agents of technological change in their respective industries. The growth of useful new technological knowledge is largely the product of what goes on inside these engineering disciplines. In the chemical sector the chemist plays the major role in the development of new products, but the design of the appropriate manufacturing technology for the new products, as well as improved technologies for manufacturing old products, are in the hands of the chemical engineers.

It turns out not to have been as easy as had originally been anticipated to explain observed behavior and outcomes in terms of the deliberate commitment of resources, on the part of maximizing agents, to capture available rents. The story of chemical engineering as a GPT is a story that is full of unintended and unexpected benefits.

There is plenty of rent seeking, especially in the behavior of oil companies which moved downstream into the chemical industry when that industry was transformed into a petrochemical industry. Furthermore, there is a prominent role played by proprietary behavior, such as patenting. Ironically, however, the most important patent – Houdry's patent on catalytic cracking – turned out to have been as important as it was because a major technological breakthrough – fluidized bed catalytic cracking – was induced by the reluctance of oil companies to pay a high royalty fee for the use of Houdry's patented invention.

But it is still difficult not to come away impressed by the failure of the oil companies to have pushed proprietary interests even farther in this burgeoning economic sector. How is one to account for that failure? There are several considerations:

1   The role played by a university was a prominent one, which meant that useful new knowledge quickly became public.
2   Much of the knowledge crucial to chemical process design was not, in any case, patentable.
3   The special features of the petroleum industry, especially the fact that the firms in this industry were large and apparently price insensitive. The emerging GPT under consideration was an increasing returns technology, and demand was growing extremely rapidly – so rapidly that firms were prepared to remain quite insensitive to price. The "name of the game," throughout the interwar years, was to increase output in response to a rapid growth in expected demand.

This chapter, then, explores the perspective that chemical engineering can be usefully thought of as a general purpose technology. GPTs have, so far, been identified as specific forms of hardware: steam engines, machine tools, dynamos, computers, etc. However, it is suggested here that the concept of a general purpose technology should not be confined to hardware. Indeed, a discipline that provides the concepts and the methodologies to generate new or improved technologies over a wide range of downstream economic activity may be thought of as an even purer, or "higher order," GPT.

This should not be controversial. A steam engine or a dynamo are not technologies; they are tangible capital equipment. "Steam" or "electricity," meaning bodies of knowledge about how to produce steam or electricity and to use them as sources of power or light in steam engines or dynamos, are technologies. Similarly, chemical engineering is a body of knowledge about the design of certain technologies: specifically, chemical engineering is a body of knowledge about the design of process plants to produce chemical or other products whose production involves chemical transformations. Since chemical engineering provides essential guidance to the design of a very wide range of plants, it may usefully be thought of as a GPT. Furthermore, there has been both a vertical and a horizontal dimension to the externalities that were generated. The emergence of chemical engineering meant that downstream sectors experienced lower invention costs. But, in addition, there was a powerful horizontal externality, in the sense that the vast market for petroleum shaped the development of petrochemicals through the intermediation of chemical engineering.

The relationship of chemical engineering to the science of chemistry

The first step in this exploration must, necessarily, be a deck-clearing operation. In order to understand the role played by chemical engineering in the process of technological change, it is necessary to deal with a widely held view that chemical engineering, like other engineering professions, is simply applied science – in this case applied chemistry. It is suggested that chemical engineering can most usefully be thought of as a body of technological knowledge that is not reducible to applied science, nor did it have its historical origins in science, although at a later stage in its development it began to draw upon certain realms of science and, in that sense, subsequently became more scientific. Chemical engineering is, rather, a body of useful knowledge concerning certain manufacturing processes that could not be derived by deduction or by simple extension from the established sciences.

Although the science of chemistry indeed became a major source of new chemical products, beginning with Perkin's immensely important opening up of the field of organic chemistry in the second half of the nineteenth century, that scientific breakthrough provided very little guidance to the process technologies that would be essential to the manufacture of chemical products in the twentieth century. Chemical engineering emerged early in the twentieth century as a separate body of knowledge that could guide the design as well as the operation of chemical process plants, including plants producing old established products, such as ammonia, in addition to new ones. But the rapid expansion of chemical engineering in the twentieth century was due not so much to the late nineteenth-century growth of the synthetic dye industries as to other industries that were far more dependent on chemical engineering capabilities.

It must be stressed, however, that chemical engineering did have critical connections with science, although these connections were quite different from the usual portrayals. As chemical engineering matured, it created a framework that eventually made it possible to exploit scientific knowledge and scientific methodologies more effectively. But such possibilities were limited at the outset. It was only when the discipline of chemical engineering reached a reasonably mature stage that it became possible to exploit science in a more systematic way. The construction of that framework, or platform, was a necessary prior step. Engineering preceded science and laid the foundations that made the utilization of science possible.

Indeed, it may not be stretching the GPT perspective excessively to say that the science of chemistry can be usefully thought of as an "applications field" of chemical engineering. I mean this in the specific sense that, once the discipline of chemical engineering had been firmly established, the prospective economic payoff to chemical research of a more basic nature was substantially raised. Consider polymer chemistry, a field that has been, for many years, dominated by research in private industry. Du Pont's willingness to finance the fundamental researches of Carothers, that led to the development of nylon, was certainly strengthened by the firm's growing confidence, based on recent advances in chemical engineering, that it could produce such new materials on a commercial scale. The point is a more general one: progress in the realm of engineering may provide powerful inducements to the performance of scientific research at a more fundamental level.

The design and construction of plants devoted to large-scale chemical processing activities involve an entirely different set of activities and capabilities than those that generated the new chemical entities in the laboratory. To begin with, such activities as mixing, heating, and contaminant control, which can be carried out with great precision in the lab, are immensely more difficult to handle in large-scale operations, especially if high levels of precision are required. Furthermore, economic considerations must obviously play a critical role in the design process. Cost considerations become decisive in an industrial context, and cost considerations are intimately connected to decisions concerning optimal scale of plant. A central feature of chemical engineering is that its practitioners have been more deeply involved in dealing with cost considerations than other engineering professions.

Thus, the discovery of a new chemical entity has commonly posed an entirely new question, one that is remote from the scientific context of the laboratory: how does one go about producing it? A chemical process plant is far from a scaled-up version of the original laboratory equipment. A simple, multiple enlargement of the dimensions of small-scale experimental equipment would be likely to yield disastrous results. Experimental equipment may have been made of glass or porcelain. A manufacturing plant will almost certainly have to be constructed of very different materials. Producing by the ton is distinctly different from producing by the ounce. This indeed is what accounts for the unique importance of the pilot plant, which may be thought of as a device for translating the findings of laboratory research into a technically feasible and economically efficient, large-scale production process.

The translation, however, requires competencies that are unlikely to exist at the experimental research level: a knowledge of mechanical engineering and physics and an understanding of the underlying economics of the alternative engineering approaches that may be available for manufacturing in large quantities.

Pilot plants (which, in recent years, have been partially replaced by computer simulation exercises), have been indispensable in attempting to predict the performance of a full-scale production plant. Pilot plants are, themselves, a technology the purpose of which is the reduction of the uncertainties that are inherent in moving to large-scale production. Until a pilot plant was built, the precise characteristics of the output could not be determined; and such essential activities as test marketing could not proceed without the availability of reliable samples. Various other features of the production process could not possibly be derived from any form of scientific knowledge alone. Consider the recycle problem. Very few chemical reactions are complete in the reaction stage. Therefore, products of the reaction stage will not only include desired end products but also intermediates, unreacted feed, and trace impurities – some measurable and some unmeasurable. Impurities, in particular, are identified by the operation of the pilot plant in order to achieve a steady state condition on a continuing basis.

It has been true of many of the most important new materials that have been introduced in the twentieth century that a gap of several, or even many years, has separated their discovery under laboratory conditions from the industrial capability to manufacture them on a commercial basis. This was true of the first polymers that W. H. Carothers had produced with his glass equipment at the du Pont Laboratories. It was also true of polyethylene, one of the most widely used new materials of the twentieth century, and terephthalic acid, an essential material in the production of terylene, a major synthetic fiber. It was in order to manage such transitions from test tubes to manufacture, where output was to be measured in tons rather than ounces, that an entirely new methodology, totally distinct from the science of chemistry, began to be devised early in the century. The new methodology involved exploiting the central concept of "unit operations." This term, coined by Arthur D. Little at MIT in 1915, provided the conceptual basis for what was to become a rigorous, quantitative approach to large-scale chemical manufacturing, and thus may be taken to mark the emergence of chemical engineering as a unique discipline, in no way reducible to "applied chemistry."

Why is it incorrect to think of technologies as simply the legitimate offspring of scientific "mother" disciplines? Scientific progress over the centuries has proceeded precisely by abstracting from problems that are at the heart of the concerns of the engineering disciplines. Physics has, for example, like other scientific disciplines, made great progress historically by confining itself to problems for which it could offer rigorous mathematical treatment and solutions. This has entailed abstracting from phenomena for which conceptual generality or rigorous solutions may be impossible. Thus, in formulating the classical laws of physics, Newton ignored the effects of friction in determining the acceleration of a falling object. Engineers, however, in designing new machinery or equipment, did not have the luxury of ignoring friction, viscosity or turbulence. They had to develop designs, and to solve problems, for which no scientific theory existed to provide guidance. Of necessity, they have therefore had recourse to experimentation with small-scale working models, but then they had to confront the sometimes awesomely complex problems involved in inferring the behavior of a projected full-scale prototype from the experimental performance of an observed, small-scale working model. How, in particular, does one adjust for "scale effects," perhaps the single most persistent challenge in chemical process plant design?

The general point is that the engineer's solution to the need for design data does not draw directly upon a scientific model, nor does the engineer's solution illuminate some more fundamental features of the phenomena under investigation. Nevertheless, the empirically derived coefficients are adequate for the design of industrial equipment that perform their required functions with a high degree of predictability and reliability. Of particular significance for present purposes, such engineering data, developed by empirical experimentation, may be of primary importance to the industrial sector, where it can be used for generating design data for prototype size by making use of dimensionless numbers. The best-known dimensionless number is the Reynolds number; using this it is possible to predict the transition from laminar to turbulent flow in an enclosed pipe or, later, for a moving object immersed in a fluid. Osborne Reynolds formulated this relationship in 1883 as a result of some ingenious experiments, and it has remained fundamental to the design of chemical process plants to this day.[4]

The emergence of chemical engineering

Where did chemical engineering first emerge? As an academic discipline the answer is clearly MIT in the second decade of the twentieth century. In fact, MIT's early intellectual leadership here was so dominant that, in order to avoid an extended treatment, the following discussion will focus exclusively on that institution.[5]

The key figure who forcefully articulated in 1915 what came to be the original unifying concept of this discipline was Arthur D. Little. The concept was that of "unit operations." Little first presented this concept, which was to become extremely influential, in a report to the Corporation of the Massachusetts Institute of Technology in December 1915, a report that also led to the establishment of the School of Chemical Engineering Practice at the Institute. In Little's words:

> Any chemical process, on whatever scale conducted, may be resolved into a coordinated series of what may be termed "unit actions," as pulverizing, mixing, heating, roasting, absorbing, condensing, lixiviating, precipitating, crystallizing, filtering, dissolving, electrolyzing and so on. The number of these basic unit operations is not very large and relatively few of them are involved in any particular process ... Chemical engineering

research ... is directed toward the improvement, control and better coordination of these unit operations and the selection or development of the equipment in which they are carried out.[6]

A critical feature of the concept of unit operations is that it made it possible at once to go far beyond the merely descriptive approach of industrial chemistry by calling attention to a small number of distinctive processes that were common to a number of industries. This act of intellectual abstraction, which Little initiated, laid the foundations for a more rigorous and, eventually, more quantitative discipline. Little looked at the chemical sector that until then had been seen as a large number of unique vertical sequences describing the manufacturing steps of individual products, and looked across these sequences horizontally, calling attention to the small number of common elements in each of them. It seems reasonable to call Little's manifesto an attempt to provide a general purpose technology to the numerous sectors of the economy that make use of chemical processing plants, although it is essential to add that this particular GPT, chemical engineering, was to provide invaluable service to product lines that had not yet been developed.

It must be noted, furthermore, that such chemical processing plants have existed in a large number of industries beyond the traditional chemical industry proper. This would include petroleum refining (of which more later), rubber, leather, coal (by-product distillation plants), many food processing industries, sugar refining, explosives, ceramics and glass, paper and pulp, cement, metallurgical industries (such as aluminum and iron and steel), etc. So, a critical part of the case for regarding chemical engineering as a general purpose technology is that the impact of the discipline went far beyond the limits of the traditional chemical industry, even before the postwar rise of the new petrochemical industries.

After the articulation of the concept of unit operations, chemical engineering was in a position to be able to accumulate a set of methodological tools that could be refined and that could provide the basis for a wide range of problem-solving activities connected with the design of chemical process plants. The awareness that there were a limited number of similar operations common to many industries served to identify research priorities and therefore to point to a disciplinary research agenda. This was not possible so long as technologists remained lost in the particularities of innumerable specific products.

Moreover, and not least important, the concept of unit operations had great pedagogical value; it provided the basis for a curriculum that could be taught. All this did not happen immediately. Rather, the establishment of a curriculum of marketable skills had to await more extensive interaction between universities and private industry. But it is not surprising that, in 1920, just a few years after Little's formulation, chemical engineering achieved the status of a separate department at MIT, under the chairmanship of W. K. Lewis. The teaching of chemical engineering was to be organized around the concept of unit operations for the next few decades, but it must be immediately added that the concept underwent substantial alteration in its intellectual content almost from the beginning.

An engineer trained in terms of unit operations could mix and match these operations as necessary in order to produce a wide variety of distinct final products. Such an engineer was much more flexible and resourceful in his approach to problem solving. Of key importance is that he was now well equipped to take techniques and methods from one branch of industry and to transfer them to other branches. Experience in one place could now be readily transferred to other, apparently unrelated, places, i.e., unrelated in terms of final products. This capability was especially valuable in the innovation process – particularly as new materials and new intermediate products emerged. Thus, research that improved the efficiency of any one process was now likely to be more quickly employed in a large number of places. Putting the point somewhat differently, the identification of a small number of unit operations common to a large number of industries meant that it was now possible to identify specific research topics where new findings could be confidently expected to experience widespread utilization, i.e., they were general purpose technologies.

The particular way in which chemical engineering was institutionalized in the US was of great importance. The university locus of research assured that the focus of intellectual progress would be on general results rather than merely the ad hoc solution of specific industrial problems. At the same time, MIT's strong link with private industry, especially its dependence on private industry for funding, assured that university research would remain focused on issues of direct relevance to industrial needs. In fact, it seems a plausible speculation that the overwhelming American leadership in the discipline of chemical engineering owed much to the especially close connections between university and industry.[7] A much more prominent role of government as a funder of research, as was the case in Europe, did lead to a very different outcome.

The maturing and expanding application of chemical engineering

In the interwar years and post World War II years, the discipline of chemical engineering underwent a huge expansion in the range of its industrial coverage and impact. This expansion was made possible by the fruitfulness of the unit operations approach – or, more precisely, by the transformation of a rather loosely defined concept into one of steadily increasing quantitative rigor.

In the years after Little's formulation of the concept of unit operations, research in chemical engineering focused heavily on acquiring a deeper understanding of each operation in order to establish mathematical regularities that would reduce the cost of the designing process as well as improve the efficiency of the equipment that was designed. Eventually these separate operations were reduced to more inclusive concepts, such as fluid mechanics and heat transfer. These concepts became more inclusive and incorporated processes based on the principles underlying the operation of gas, liquid, or solid components in different concentrations.[8]

In time, chemical engineers attempted to codify the basic physics underlying momentum (viscous flow), energy transport (heat conduction, convection, and radiation), and mass transport (diffusion).[9] It was continued advances like these that have led recently to the claim that chemical engineering has achieved the status of an "engineering science." As a result, much of the designing activity of chemical engineers is now understood at a more fundamental level, while the design of chemical processing equipment still draws upon empirical regularities that have stood the test of time.

But the success, and indeed the transformation of the discipline, owed an enormous debt to two exogenous events. The first was World War I which brought in its wake a great expansion in the demand for chemical engineers to supply the munitions, nitrates, gasoline, and other requirements of a wartime economy (including chemical warfare).[10]

Whereas the number of students attending chemical engineering courses in the United States remained far behind those in electrical engineering and mechanical engineering before the war, the number expanded rapidly in the second decade of the century, growing by more than 60 per cent between 1916 and 1918 alone, and rising to almost 6,000 in 1920–1.[11]

The second and more enduring exogenous event was the spectacular growth in the automobile industry, with its voracious appetite for liquid fuel. There were fewer than 500,000 registered cars in the US in 1910, but over 8,000,000 in 1920 and over 23,000,000 in 1930, by which time the automobile industry was the largest manufacturing industry, in terms of value added, in the US.[12] After 1920 the history of chemical engineering became simply inseparable from the history of petroleum refining. The new technologies and new methodological skills developed by the chemical engineering profession in satisfying the demand for gasoline eventually had enormous unanticipated consequences. The usefulness of these capabilities multiplied when, after World War II, first the US chemical industry and then the world chemical industry shifted their resource base to petroleum feedstocks, creating the present-day petrochemical industry. America had substantial commercial advantages in the petrochemical industry. There were vast domestic deposits of petroleum, and this country had, at an early date, explored technological alternatives for petroleum refining. In doing so, it acquired chemical engineering capabilities in that activity that later "spilled over" from petroleum refining to petrochemicals. In this sense, resource endowment indeed mattered, but it mattered in large part because it served as a powerful stimulus to acquire technological capabilities that simply did not exist in 1920. America's early experience in petroleum refining served to provide powerful first mover learning advantages when the world later turned to petrochemicals.

With that transition, the technologies that had been specifically developed for the refining of petroleum eventually came to provide the technological basis for an expanding share of the world's industrial output. Skills that were initially acquired in petroleum refining were later transferred to the much larger canvas of the emerging petrochemical industry, including major new product categories such as plastics, synthetic fibers, and synthetic rubber. The "crash" program to develop synthetic rubber during World War II was almost entirely the achievement of chemical engineers. But many of the new capabilities spilled over into inorganic chemical products as well. This new technology, and the broader design and problem-solving skills that were responsible for them, also exercised an impact well beyond the chemical industry. In addition to the beneficiaries mentioned earlier, chemical engineers eventually became responsible for the processing of uranium for nuclear power plants. They were also responsible for developing the manufacturing technology of submerged fermentation that made penicillin available during World War II.

Thus, in attacking the problems of large-scale refining of petroleum, chemical engineers created a vastly expanded pool of design and problem-solving capabilities that were critical to the creation of some entirely new industries, as well as making it possible to shift from batch production to large-volume production methods, in the form of continuous processing, in a number of existing industries. At the same time, it also made a substantial contribution to the whole realm of automatic control because, although continuous processing plants already existed in certain places before the advent of automatic controls, these controls raised considerably the productivity of such plants. Continuous cracking technology, when introduced in the 1920s, could achieve far higher levels of throughputs when the continuous cracking process plants were operated with automatic controls.[13]

Seen from the perspective of the 1990s, the intimate linkage between the petroleum and chemical industries seems "natural" and therefore inevitable. But from the vantage point of 1920 that was emphatically not so. The "natural" connection between the two industries was, in reality, a complex human creation involving the mobilization of vast amounts of resources and the sustained exercise of human intelligence in the development of inventions, novel designs, and a wide range of new problem-solving methodologies. Before the invention of the internal combustion engine, petroleum was valued primarily as an illuminant and a lubricant, and the more volatile fractions were commonly disposed of as waste. It became a major source of fuel for transportation purposes *only* as a result of the invention of the automobile. And the technologies that chemical engineering developed, in order to extract fuel from petroleum, provided much of the technological basis for a far larger group of industries – petrochemical industries – in the postwar years. Indeed, to emphasize once more, the new technological capabilities also spilled over into many sectors outside of both petrochemicals and the older chemical industries.

In 1920 the state of technological knowledge was such that petroleum was not regarded as a significant input into the chemical industry. The chemical industry thought of its inputs in terms of chemicals in a less processed state, on the one hand, and feed-stocks drawn from coke oven by-products, on the other. It was only as the result of extensive research and the slow accumulation of technical knowledge that the oil companies came to realize that their refining operations could produce, not just fuel and lubricants, but organic chemical intermediates as well.[14] In the 1920s, the offgases of oil refineries, if they were not simply flared, were likely to be employed only as fuel, a low-value use, at the refineries themselves. The transformation of the chemical industry, as it existed in 1920, into the petrochemical industry that matured in the post World War II years, was in large measure the achievement of the chemical engineering profession. It was a process in which by-products that were formerly treated as waste materials were converted into sources of great commercial value.[15] In a sense this was a replay of an earlier development in nineteenth-century Germany when a by-product derived from coke ovens, coal tar, provided the raw material basis for a burgeoning synthetic dye industry. And it would be no exaggeration to say that Standard Oil Company of New Jersey and Shell were induced to undertake the research that brought them from petroleum refining into the chemical industry by their growing awareness of the commercial opportunities that might flow from the eventual utilization of the waste products of their refinery operations.[16]

The role of MIT

This achievement involved a uniquely intimate set of interactions between the petroleum refining industry and the newly formed chemical engineering department at MIT. During the 1920s that department built upon the conceptual platform of unit operations that had been introduced by Arthur D. Little. But that concept needs to be understood as the inevitably crude starting point of the discipline of chemical engineering, and not as its terminus. In fact, the concept was enriched and deepened very quickly as MIT's chemical engineers confronted the difficulties of satisfying the demand for gasoline. The technique of thermal cracking was first introduced by Standard Oil in 1913 (the Burton process). Thermal cracking was far cheaper than the "straight-run" distillation method that it replaced ("straight-run" refers to the refinery streams obtained from the fractional distillation process), and was to remain totally dominant in petroleum refining until just before World War II.

Thermal cracking was analyzed with increasing sophistication, in terms of its specific unit operations, including heat transfer, fluid flow, and distillation.[17] The design process was approached in increasingly quantitative rather than crudely empirical terms. In the early 1930s, for example, pressure-volume-temperature relationships for gas mixtures were established that were sufficiently accurate for the design of refining equipment, and this knowledge proved to be useful elsewhere.[18]

Undoubtedly the leading academic contributor was W. K. Lewis, the chairman of MIT's chemical engineering department, who served as a consultant to Standard Oil of New Jersey (later Exxon) for many years (Exxon Research and Engineering had been founded in 1919). Lewis' first efforts at Standard Oil were to provide precision distillation equipment and to convert batch processing methods to methods that were both continuous and automatic, as in thermal cracking (the so-called "tube-and-tank" process) and continuous vacuum distillation. In doing these things he was also, unknowingly of course, inventing technologies upon which the petrochemical industries of the future were to be based.

Distillation is the most important single activity in petroleum refining. Lewis and his MIT colleagues during the 1930s "advanced the theory of fractional distillation to the point at which equipment could be designed that would split multicomponent hydrocarbon streams predictably and consistently into the desired fractions."[19] By 1924 Lewis had helped to achieve a significant increase in oil recovery by the use of vacuum stills. (Between 1914 and 1927 the average yield of gasoline rose from 18 to 36 per cent of crude throughput.) This work and his earlier bubble tower designs became refinery standards.

At the same time, however, course work at MIT was quickly expanded to embody these new concepts and their underlying design principles. Lewis, along with two colleagues (William Walker and William McAdams) published the first edition of what was to be an immensely influential textbook, *Principles of Chemical Engineering*, in 1923. It was a text that took a long step forward from A. D. Little's initial formulation of unit operations to a methodology of far greater quantitative and mathematical rigor. In this respect it provided a much-improved platform for the introduction into chemical engineering research of scientific concepts such as thermodynamics. Indeed, thermodynamics and transport phenomena are now engineering concepts at the heart of the discipline of chemical engineering.

In the late 1920s, Exxon negotiated a series of agreements with the German chemical giant, IG Farben, that would provide access to their extensive research on hydrogenation and synthetic substitutes for oil and rubber from coal. It was also anticipated that the German findings might be used to increase gasoline yields and promote Exxon's entry into chemicals. In putting together a new research group for this purpose, Lewis was again consulted. He recommended Robert Haslam, head of the MIT Chemical Engineering Practice School. Haslam, on leave from MIT, formed a team of fifteen MIT staff members and graduates who set up a research organization in Baton Rouge, Louisiana. Many of the members of this group later rose to positions of eminence in petroleum and chemicals.[20]

Much of what subsequently took place in modern petroleum processing until World War II originated in Baton Rouge, and the primary responsibility for these achievements was the solid phalanx of MIT chemical engineers who worked there. With the continuing advice of Lewis, and later (in 1935) of MIT Professor Edwin R. Gilliland, Baton Rouge produced such outstanding process developments as hydroforming, fluid flex coking, and fluidized bed catalytic cracking. This last innovation, a contribution to petroleum refining that was to play a major role in World War II, and was to dominate the refining of petroleum in the postwar world, also ultimately became the most important processing technology for propylene and butane feedstocks in the chemical industry. Catalytic cracking plants provided the essential raw materials for the "crash" program for the production of synthetic rubber in World War II. They also provided the high octane gasoline that significantly improved allied fighter aircraft performance. The key patent was originally applied for by Professors W. K. Lewis and E. R. Gilliland in January 1940 and assigned to Standard Oil Development Company.[21]

Lewis, as a chemical engineer, adopted an overall, systems approach to the design of continuous automated processing plants for the refining of petroleum. This approach, and many of the specific design ingredients, was to shape much of the later technology of the world petrochemical industry. Petroleum refining thus provided vitally important learning experiences in the design of the continuous flow, automated processing technology that was later transferred to the much more diversified canvas of petrochemicals in the postwar years – plastics, synthetic fibers, synthetic rubber.[22]

It is important to stress the intimacy of the interface between the consulting activities of the chemical engineering faculty and the training of future chemical engineers at MIT. Faculty encountered research problems in their consulting activities and brought these problems back to the Institute where students might pursue their possible solutions under faculty supervision. Problems encountered in the course of faculty consulting were likely to appear on their lists of suggested thesis topics.[23] On some occasions, at least, their solutions were momentous for industry.

Consider the development of fluidized bed catalytic cracking. Fluidized bed technology was just one of the ways in which chemical engineers rendered chemical processing continuous. But it was probably the most important, single continuous process innovation. Petroleum "cracking" techniques make it possible to break large, heavy hydrocarbon molecules into smaller and lighter ones. Catalytic cracking technology made possible a much higher degree of control over the output that could be extracted from a given quantity of petroleum. In practice, this meant raising the yield of higher-priced gasoline that could be derived from the heavier crude oil fractions, an achievement of enormous economic significance.

Although Houdry had introduced the use of a catalyst in petroleum refining in the late 1930s, his fixed bed catalytic process, while a major breakthrough, suffered from a serious limitation. It deposited carbon on the catalyst, leading to rapid degeneration, and required regeneration. This depositing of carbon led to severe deactivation in ten or twenty minutes. In short, the Houdry process was not continuous. There was also a very different, but far from trivial problem: Houdry was asking for a very high licensing fee.

Although the Houdry process was already being commercialized in the late 1930s, Exxon (then Standard Oil) decided to search for the development of a more efficient process of their own. After numerous engineering studies, it was concluded that there were inherent and insuperable limitations in a cyclic, fixed-bed design. Consequently, the focus of research was shifted to circulating catalytic systems that would permit continuous operation.

> In 1938, Drs. W. K. Lewis and E. R. Gilliland of MIT's Chemical Engineering Department, in their role as consultants to Standard Oil Development Company, suggested that the tube in which the reaction took place should be vertical rather than horizontal. They were asked to investigate the behavior of finely

divided particles in vertical tubes and so initiated a research program at MIT. Two graduate students, John Chambers and Scott Walker, carried out the experiments and derived some of the basic engineering relationships underlying the fluid technique . . . The Standard Oil Development Company realized that the fluid technique offered an excellent mechanism for manipulating the catalyst and oil streams and quickly took over the research. The students at MIT had worked with air and catalyst mixtures alone, but within six months the Development Company was cracking oil in the presence of a fluid catalyst.[24]

Thus, fluidized bed catalytic cracking was largely the joint achievement of MIT and the Esso laboratories. The purely theoretical work and laboratory-scale experiments were performed primarily at MIT, while the initial problem formulation and the later scaled-up pilot plant experiments were carried out by private industry. (Other contributors to fluid catalytic cracking included Universal Oil Products Company, Kellogg Company, Texas Development Corporation, Gulf Research Development Company, and Shell Oil Company.)

The principles of fluidization, developed in the specific context of petroleum refining, were subsequently to experience extensive applications in other types of chemical processing, not only in the newly emerging petrochemical industries, but also over a much broader spectrum of chemical processing activities. The research carried out jointly between MIT and Exxon on the flow properties of powdered solids suspended in gases turned out to have a much larger relevance. "Potentially, the fluid technique has application to any process in which (1) large quantities of heat are transferred; (2) large quantities of solids must be circulated; or (3) very intimate contact between gases and solids is desired."[25] In fact, the potential uses are so great as to constitute the introduction of an entirely new unit operation.

By 1962 it was estimated that there were 350 fluidized-bed processing units throughout the world outside the petroleum industry.[26] At the same time, within the petroleum industry, a technique that had been developed for the specific purpose of catalytic cracking was also being used in fluid-bed coking, catalyst regeneration, platforming, and ethylene manufacture.[27]

A basic advantage of the fluidized-solids technique was the uniformity that it achieved with respect to particle-size distribution as well as temperature and heat transfer characteristics throughout the entire fluidized bed. This made it possible to establish precise conditions of control comparable to what could presumably be achieved before only in the laboratory. The central point is that it made possible continuous process activities for a wide variety of end uses in other industries. The technique also represented a vast improvement with respect to ease of handling.[28]

The rise of the petrochemical industry

The rise of the petrochemical industry began with the entry of a few companies, particularly Union Carbide, Shell, Dow, and Exxon, not long before the outbreak of World War II. These firms soon encountered the need for chemical engineering skills as the increasing scale of operations forced resort to continuous processing, just as it had previously in the petroleum refining industry. The techniques and skills formerly developed for the refining industry could now be applied to the demands of the petrochemical industry, as chemical raw materials began the epochal shift from coal-based to petroleum-based feedstocks. To be sure, it was not a simple shift. The problems in manufacturing chemicals were different, and in many respects even more challenging, involving corrosion, complex product separations, and purifications, toxic wastes, and hazards, etc. But the prior experience with petroleum refining provided a vast storehouse of concepts, methodologies and, not least, experience upon which the chemical engineering profession could draw. In several cases, the early entrants consisted of oil companies going downstream to capture the newly available rents.

Although the episode is not well known, the skills of the chemical engineer in the use of pilot plants and experimental design also played a crucial role in the wartime introduction of penicillin. Even though Alexander Fleming's brilliant insight (that a common bread mold could be responsible for the bactericidal effect that he observed in his Petri dish) was made in 1928, penicillin still remained unavailable at the outbreak of World War II. Producing penicillin on a very large commercial scale during that war required a "crash program" in which the production problems were solved not, as would normally have been expected, by the pharmaceutical chemist but by chemical engineers designing and operating a pilot plant. The chemical engineers demonstrated how the technique of aerobic submerged fermentation, which became the dominant production technology, could be made to work by solving the complex problems of heat and mass transfer.[29]

There is a revealing aspect to the wartime development of penicillin that is also worth observing. Although the British clearly pioneered the scientific research leading to the development of penicillin, their main subsequent research interest was in finding new uses for penicillin and in improving its effectiveness in the clinical treatment of infection. In Germany, on the other hand, where there was a very strong tradition and accumulation of skills in chemical synthesis, the synthesis route was the preferred approach. As it was later established, this route was much more difficult and costly than obtaining the penicillin directly from the mold.[30] In America, by contrast, as soon as the significance of penicillin was fully appreciated, the skills of the chemical engineer were enlisted to identify efficient ways of achieving large-scale production methods and increased yields. The joint achievement of the chemical engineer and the microbiologist should perhaps best be described as the first great achievement of biochemical engineering.

The maturing of the discipline of chemical engineering also gave rise to an important organizational innovation that was to accelerate the diffusion of new chemical processing technologies: specialized engineering firms (SEFs). The skills in designing continuous-flow, automated processes, first acquired in petroleum refining, could be, and were, exploited on a world-wide scale in the postwar years. Since the development of new chemical products was largely in the hands of big firms which performed the necessary R&D, there existed an important niche that could be filled by small firms consisting of well-trained chemical engineers who could concentrate their efforts exclusively on the design of chemical process plants. A large petrochemical firm that designed its own equipment was severely limited in its ability to benefit from accumulating experience, since the need to do such designing for its own internal purposes was, at best, only intermittent. On the other hand, small, specialized chemical engineering firms, working for a potentially large, indeed world-wide market, had numerous opportunities for improving both their designing and innovating capabilities by designing particular plants many times for a succession of different clients.[31] Indeed, the feedback of know-how from a succession of clients was a major source of technological learning and competitive advantage to the most successful specialized engineering firms, such as the Scientific Design Company.

Perhaps even more important was the rapid diffusion of recently acquired technological knowledge that resulted from the activities of the SEFs. These firms played an especially significant role in developing and licensing processing technologies, thus enabling newcomers such as Conoco, Arco, and Amoco to enter the petrochemical industry in the 1960s and 1970s, and to do so with, for example, ethylene plants that were at least as efficient as those already being operated by the traditional large producers.[32] In effect, SEFs represented a new pattern of specialization in which certain firms thrived by becoming the vehicles for rapidly diffusing or "externalizing" the new technologies developed in petroleum refining.

Some concluding observations

Back in the 1920s, the newly established discipline of chemical engineering set about the business of designing more efficient processing technologies in order to satisfy the rapidly expanding demand for gasoline. In achieving this end, I suggest that it also went a long way toward developing the processing technologies that were to be essential to the vast expansion of the petrochemical industries, beginning around the time of World War II. In doing this, the discipline of chemical engineering became, in effect, a general purpose technology.

Of course, chemical engineering did not become a general purpose technology entirely through its own actions. Although this chapter has emphasized the growing needs of the automobile in stimulating the growth of chemical engineering, its expansion to the status of a general purpose technology required the later growth of the downstream industries that would expand the range of productive operations to which the technologies of the chemical engineer might be applied. Chemical engineering became a GPT, in large measure, when research in polymer chemistry (Staudinger, Meyer, Mark, Carothers) laid the scientific basis for a whole range of new products that could best be produced from petroleum feedstocks. The scientific basis for these new products that were to dominate the petrochemical industry – plastics, synthetic fiber, synthetic rubber – was also, like chemical engineering, a product of the interwar years. But these petrochemical industries only acquired major economic significance in the years after World War II.

This chronology points to an interesting, serendipitous feature of chemical engineering as a general purpose technology. The GPT capability did not emerge in response to the prior existence of a large, heterogeneous body of downstream users of the technology, whose existence generated strong economic incentives to upstream suppliers of complementary inputs. Complementarities were, indeed, of central importance. However, the story of chemical engineering as a GPT is one in which the general purpose capability was developed primarily in response to the needs of one sector: petroleum. Only later on did petroleum come to constitute the main feedstock for an expanding multiplicity of industrial users. Thus, developments upstream in the interwar years clearly preceded the extensive developments downstream that eventually transformed chemical engineering into a GPT. The story is one of large unanticipated benefits in which a capability originally developed for one limited set of needs turned out to satisfy a much larger set of needs – needs that only developed later.

A critical achievement of the initial concept of unit operations is that it had clarified the objectives of research. In this sense, it served as what has been called, in a somewhat different context, a focusing device. Moreover, by providing an intellectual platform for science, it eventually altered the nature of the platform itself. Thus, chemical engineering did not emerge out of prior science; rather, as it matured, chemical engineering strengthened the opportunities for focusing scientific concepts and methodologies upon the problems with which it dealt. As a result, it eventually became more scientific.

This chapter has emphasized the crucial role that one institution of higher education, MIT, played in the rise of chemical engineering. Some further aspects of the impact of that role ought to be made more explicit. As we have seen, the interface between MIT and private industry was a very intimate one, with professors serving as regular consultants over extended periods of time in dealing with the problems of petroleum refining. So long as professors maintained an active role in a teaching capacity, they were under a natural pressure to place the knowledge, acquired from their specific problem-solving activities as consultants, in a larger and more general context. This meant fitting that knowledge together in an internally consistent way with other knowledge in their discipline. In brief, when reverting to their teaching roles, faculty needed to systematize their knowledge, a natural and essential precondition for the writing of textbooks as well as other forms of publication. This had profound implications for the diffusion of new technological knowledge, not just because open universities "naturally" diffuse their knowledge, but because the need to systematize knowledge for teaching purposes meant that faculty had to spend time and sustained effort in further activities that inevitably facilitated the spread of useful knowledge.

Thus, the story that is recounted here is not reducible to a simple model of human agents driven by maximizing behavior. Rather, a crucial part of the story involves the ways in which the institutional location of one group of actors – university professors – led to a more complex pattern of behavior. It was this location, and not just maximizing behavior, that brought about the emergence of a new academic discipline. And this academic discipline, in turn, generated not only the expected "vertical" externalities of lower downstream invention costs; it also generated a "horizontal" externality when the growing demand for refined petroleum products led to the training of an enlarged cohort of chemical engineers who, in turn, shaped the creation of a huge petrochemical industry.

To put this argument in a deliberately exaggerated form: this petrochemical industry was more the achievement of du Pont than of Exxon. Exxon "merely" increased the supply and reduced the price of petroleum, whereas du Pont employed the discipline of chemical engineering to introduce and to produce a vastly expanded array of new products that utilized the cheaper petroleum inputs.[33]

The prominent role played by an academic institution devoted to teaching as well as research was of great importance for another, and related, reason. All students, whatever their eventual professional affiliation, were taught the common language of chemical engineering. Thus, even though they went to work in different firms or organizations, they had all been taught common concepts, theories, and methods. This vastly reduced the barriers to the diffusion of technical knowledge across organizational boundary lines. It therefore facilitated the development of a professional community of people who could communicate easily with one another. Indeed, this would appear to be a peculiar feature of a discipline as a GPT, as opposed to a piece of hardware as a GPT. It was what made chemical engineers, after the introduction of the concept of unit operations, so different from the earlier industrial chemists, who tended to speak in very distinct, idiosyncratic, industry-specific or even firm-specific languages. To some extent, this would appear to be what happened in Germany, where chemical engineering did not emerge as a distinct subject until after World War II, when it was essentially borrowed from America. In Germany, universities played an important role in training many students in chemistry, but these chemists knew no engineering, and therefore required extensive on-the-job training in the different chemical divisions of the firms in which they were eventually employed. It seems likely that this led to more secrecy and less extensive interfirm communication in Germany.[34]

The notion of a general purpose technology has, up until now, been confined to machines or devices that were utilized over some broad range of productive activities. I suggest that extension of the concept to include intellectual disciplines, such as chemical engineering, may bring with it valuable new insights into the underlying determinants of technological change and the diffusion of new technologies. As suggested at the outset, a distinctive feature of the Second Industrial Revolution has been the emergence of new engineering disciplines that have become the centers of technological learning and, subsequently, the carriers of technological change to their respective industries. In this sense, studying the development and functioning of these disciplines offers the enticing prospect of penetrating to a deeper level of understanding of the sources of technological dynamism of industrial economies.

Finally, by extending the concept of general purpose technologies to engineering disciplines, that concept can vastly strengthen the New Growth Theory at what is its most critical and, at the same time, perhaps its weakest link: accounting for the growth of useful knowledge.

Notes

1 Joseph Schumpeter and the economic interpretation of history

1 J. Schumpeter, *Capitalism, Socialism and Democracy*, London, Unwin University Books, 1952, p. xiv. The book was first published in 1942 by Harper & Brothers, New York.

2 J. Schumpeter, *History of Economic Analysis*, New York, Oxford University Press, 1954, pp. 12–13. The italics are Schumpeter's. The book was edited from manuscript by Elizabeth Boody Schumpeter.

3 Schumpeter, *Capitalism, Socialism and Democracy*, p. 44. The italics are Schumpeter's.

4 Ibid., pp. 11–12.

5 J. Schumpeter, *The Theory of Economic Development*, Cambridge, Mass., Harvard University Press, 1949, p. 12. The book was first published in German in 1911 and translated by Redvers Opie.

6 Schumpeter, *Capitalism, Socialism and Democracy*, p. 12.

7 Ibid., pp. 12–13.

8 Ibid., pp. 129–30.

9 Schumpeter, *Theory of Economic Development*, pp. 62, 63.

10 As reprinted in R. Clemence (ed.), *Essays of J. A. Schumpeter*, Cambridge, Mass., Addison-Wesley, 1951, pp. 158–60.

11 Ibid., p. 160. The locus classicus for the application of the evolutionary concept to economic change in recent years is, of course, R. Nelson and S. Winter, *An Evolutionary Theory of Economic Change*, Cambridge, Mass., Harvard University Press, 1982.

12 Schumpeter, *Capitalism, Socialism and Democracy*, p. 162.

13 Ibid., pp. 82–3.

14 Ibid., p. 85, footnote 4.

15 Ibid., pp. 84–5.

16 J. Schumpeter, "The Communist Manifesto in Sociology and Economics," *Journal of Political Economy*, vol. 57, no. 3, June 1949, p. 210. The italics are Schumpeter's.

17 Schumpeter, *Capitalism, Socialism and Democracy*, p. 125.

18 Ibid., pp. 125–6.

19 Schumpeter, *Theory of Economic Development*, p. 65. Schumpeter makes
essentially the same point in other places. See, for example, J. Schumpeter, *Business Cycles: A Theoretical, Historical and Statistical Analysis of the Capitalist Process*, vol. 1, New York, McGraw-Hill Book Co.
Inc., 1939, p. 73. For Schumpeter's insistence that economists should
address the determinants of changing consumer preferences rather
than simply making endless obeisances to the virtues of free consumer
choice, see J. Schumpeter, "English Economists and the State-Managed
Economy," *Journal of Political Economy*, vol. 57, no. 5, October
1949, pp. 271–382.
20 Schumpeter, *Business Cycles*, vol. 1, p. 73.
21 See J. Schmookler, *Invention and Economic Growth*, Cambridge,
Mass., Harvard University Press, 1966.
22 See G. Stigler and G. Becker, "De Gustibus non Est Disputandum," *American Economic Review*, vol. 67, no. 2, March 1977, pp. 76–90.
23 Schumpeter, "English Economists and the State-Managed Economy,"
p. 305.
24 Schumpeter, *Capitalism, Socialism and Democracy*, p. 77.
25 Ibid., footnote 5.
26 Schumpeter, "Capitalism in the Postwar World," in Clemence, *Essays
of J. A. Schumpeter*, p. 174.
27 Schumpeter, *History of Economic Analysis*, p. 968.
28 As reprinted, in translation from the Japanese, by I. Nakayama and
S. Tobata, in Clemence, *Essays of J. A. Schumpeter*, p. 2.
29 Schumpeter, *Capitalism, Socialism and Democracy*, Part III.
30 N. Rosenberg, "Economic Experiments," *Industrial and Corporate
Change*, vol. 1, no. 1, 1992.
31 Schumpeter, *Business Cycles*, p. 187.
32 Ibid., pp. 229–30.

2 Endogeneity in twentieth-century science and technology

1 J. Schumpeter, "The Communist Manifesto in Sociology and Economics," *Journal of Political Economy*, vol. 57, no. 3, June 1949, p. 210.
2 For some interesting speculations on the subject of national support for
scientific research, see J. Schmookler, "Catastrophe and Utilitarianism
in the Development of Basic Science," in R. Tybout (ed.), *Economics
of Research and Development*, Columbus, Ohio State University Press,
1965.
3 See P. Romer, "Endogenous Technological Change," *Journal of Political
Economy*, vol. 98, no. 5, October 1990, pp. S71–S102. In employing
the term "endogenous" to embrace the work of Marx and Schumpeter
as well as the recent work of Romer and others writing within the framework of the New Growth Theory, I am using that term in the broadest
sense. In the context of economic discussions, I mean by "endogenous"
that certain outcomes (e.g., the availability of new technologies) need
to be understood as the result of purposive actions undertaken by decision makers who are responding to market forces in the pursuit of profit
maximization. This definition encompasses the contributions of the New

Growth Theory as well as the work of Marx and Schumpeter, although Marx and Schumpeter obviously addressed issues in very different domains. Moreover, they were interested specifically in accounting for changes that took place over the course of real historical time. Neither, in addition, attempted to develop their arguments within the framework of a formal mathematical model. Nevertheless, I believe that both Marx and Schumpeter would have accepted the first two premises of Romer's theoretical approach. Romer states as his first premise "that technological change . . . lies at the heart of economic growth." His second premise "is that technological change arises in large part because of intentional actions taken by people who respond to market incentives. Thus the model is one of endogenous rather than exogenous technological change" (ibid., p. S72). Marx and Schumpeter would surely have agreed.

4 The final chapter of this book, "Chemical engineering as a general purpose technology," will return to some of these issues from a different perspective.

5 See the valuable survey by P. Stephan, "The Economics of Science," *Journal of Economic Literature*, vol. 34, no. 3, September 1996, pp. 1,199–235, and P. Dasgupta and P. David, "Toward a New Economics of Science," in *Research Policy*, vol. 23, no. 5, September 1994.

6 With respect to the last-mentioned, the economics of crime, it turns out of course that crime pays, especially when the likelihood of apprehension and punishment are both low!

7 See F. Bacon, *Novum Organum*, Oxford, Clarendon Press, 1878.

8 See N. Rosenberg, "Why Do Firms Do Basic Research with Their Own Money?" *Research Policy*, vol. 19, 1990.

9 See N. Rosenberg and R. Nelson, "American Universities and Technical Advance in Industry," *Research Policy*, vol. 23, 1994, pp. 323–48.

10 R. Merton, *The Sociology of Science: Theoretical and Empirical Investigations*, Chicago, University of Chicago Press, 1973.

11 Dasgupta and David, "Toward a New Economics of Science."

12 K. Arrow, "Economic Welfare and the Allocation of Resources for Invention," in R. Nelson (ed.), *The Rate and Direction of Inventive Activity*, NBER, Princeton, N.J., Princeton University Press, 1962.

13 See D. Mowery, "Industrial Research, and Firm Size, Survival, and Growth in American Manufacturing, 1921–1946: An Assessment," *Journal of Economic History*, vol. 43, no. 4, December 1983, pp. 953–80; D. Mowery, "The Boundaries of the US Firm in R&D," in N. R. Lamoreaux and D. M. G. Raff (eds.), *Coordination and Information: Historical Perspectives on the Organization of Enterprise*, Chicago, University of Chicago Press, 1995; and D. Mowery and N. Rosenberg, *Technology and the Pursuit of Economic Growth*, New York, Cambridge University Press, 1989.

14 See Chapter 3 for more details.

15 N. Rosenberg, "How Exogenous is Science?" in N. Rosenberg, *Inside the Black Box: Technology and Economics*, New York, Cambridge University Press, 1982.

16 For a comparative analysis of these issues, see the various country

studies in R. Nelson (ed.), *National Innovation Systems*, New York, Oxford University Press, 1993.

17 See Chapter 5.

18 See R. Nelson and N. Rosenberg, "Technical Innovation and National Systems," in Nelson, *National Innovation Systems*, ch. 1; and S. Kline and N. Rosenberg, "An Overview of Innovation," in R. Landau and N. Rosenberg (eds.), *The Positive Sum Strategy*, Washington, D.C., National Academy Press, 1986.

19 Rosenberg, "Why Do Firms Do Basic Research with Their Own Money?"

20 See D. Hounshell and J. K. Smith, *Science and Corporate Strategy*, New York, Cambridge University Press, 1988, for an authoritative account of scientific research at du Pont.

21 See J. D. Bernal, *Science and Industry in the Nineteenth Century*, London, Routledge & Kegan Paul, 1953, ch. 4; and N. Rosenberg, *Technology and American Economic Growth*, New York, Harper and Row, 1972.

22 For further discussion, see N. Rosenberg, "The Growing Role of Science in the Innovation Process," in Carl Gustaf Bernhard *et al.* (eds.), *Science, Technology and Society in the Time of Alfred Nobel*, Oxford, Pergamon Press, 1982; and Rosenberg, *Technology and American Economic Growth*, pp. 18–24.

23 D. Barnett and R. Crandall, *Up from the Ashes: The Rise of the Steel Minimill in the US*, Washington, D.C., Brookings Institution, 1986.

24 For an extended treatment of the role of technological change in expanding the resource base of the forest products industry, see "Understanding the Adoption of New Technology in the Forest Products Industry," in N. Rosenberg *et al.*, *Exploring the Black Box*, Cambridge, Cambridge University Press, 1994, ch. 12.

25 P. David and G. Wright, "The Origins of American Resource Abundance," IIASA working paper 96–15, February 1996, pp. 1–2. See also Rosenberg, *Technology and American Economic Growth*, chs. 1 and 2.

26 See the highly influential report to the President of the United States by Vannevar Bush, *Science: The Endless Frontier*, Washington, D.C., USGPO, 1945.

27 *Directory of American Research and Technology*. 1992, New Providence, N.J., R. R. Bowker, 26th edition.

28 For a more extended discussion of these issues, see Rosenberg, "How Exogenous is Science?"

29 Rosenberg, *Inside the Black Box*, p. 155.

30 For a detailed account, see M. Riordan and L. Hoddeson, *Crystal Fire*, New York, W. W. Norton and Company, 1997.

31 E. Braun and S. MacDonald, *Revolution in Miniature*, New York, Cambridge University Press, 1978, p. 127.

32 "Physics through the 1990s," *Scientific Interfaces and Technological Applications*, Washington, D.C., National Academy Press, 1986; and J. L. Bromberg, *The Laser in America: 1950–1970*, Cambridge, Mass., MIT Press, 1991.

33 *Stanford University Bulletin*, 1997–8, p. 244. The influence of the "Fellow–Mentor" program, as an arrangement for drawing talented students into industrial employment, should not be underestimated.

34 N. Rosenberg, "Scientific Instrumentation and University Research," in Rosenberg, *Exploring the Black Box*, ch. 13.

3 American universities as endogenous institutions

1 In 1993, 57 per cent of all doctoral degrees awarded by US universities in engineering fields were earned by non-US citizens; in mathematics and computer science the figure was 47 per cent. See National Science Board, *Science and Engineering Indicators*, 1996, Washington, D.C., pp. 2–3. See also National Science Board, *Science and Engineering Indicators* – 1998, Arlington, Va., 1998.

2 According to an NSF report, American colleges and universities performed 51 per cent of all basic research that was projected for the year 1996. However, if one adds to that figure the basic research performed by the Federally Financed Research and Development Centers (FFRDCs), which are university-administered, the share of basic research carried out in academic centers rises to 61 per cent. See National Science Foundation, *National Patterns of R&D Resources: 1996, An SRS Special Report*, Arlington, Va., National Science Foundation, 1996.

3 For a valuable discussion of some of the relevant issues, see D. Kennedy, "Basic Research in the Universities: How Much Utility?" in R. Landau and N. Rosenberg (eds.), *The Positive Sum Strategy*, Washington, D.C., National Academy Press, 1986.

4 It should be added that higher education in Germany has long been under the control of the Lander, a situation that offers the possibility of more academic mobility and decentralization (polycentrism) than has prevailed in highly centralized systems such as France and Italy.

Schumpeter's decision to leave Germany for Harvard was brought to a climax by his failure to receive either of the two appointments that became available in Berlin in 1931–2. For an account of the complex cross currents and maneuvering between the Berlin professoriate and the Prussian Ministry of Education, see R. Allen, *Opening Doors*, New Brunswick, Transaction Publishers, vol. 1, 1991, pp. 287–91. Allen concludes that Schumpeter "probably wanted an offer only so he could turn it down" (p. 291) but presents no evidence to support this speculation.

5 A portion of a *New York Times* article on electronic commerce, November 3, 1997, reads as follows:

> Electronic commerce still eludes precise definitions. Generally, though, it refers to the way the Internet and the World Wide Web are transforming thousands of businesses around the world, allowing new kinds of interactions among companies and their suppliers and customers, as well as with their employees.
>
> For decades, business schools have prepared their students for a corporate world that was organized around function-defined departments, leading to concentrations in finance, management, marketing,

production, accounting, human resources and so on. But the Internet is changing or even eliminating these old organizational schemes.

And so a growing number of universities and graduate schools are creating curriculums to reflect these changes. Some, like the Owen School of Management at Vanderbilt University in Nashville and the University of Texas at Austin, are emerging as premier study centers for electronic commerce.

Others in this new field include the Fuqua School of Business at Duke University; Harvard College; the Sloan School at the MIT; Stanford University; the University of Michigan, and the University of Rochester.

American business schools, not surprisingly, have long been conspicuous in the speed of their curriculum development. As Alfred Chandler has observed, "In 1900 accounting courses were given in only 12 institutions of higher learning, and these courses were little more than surveys of commercial bookkeeping. By 1910, 52 colleges and universities offered accounting courses, and by 1916 the number had risen to 116." A. D. Chandler, Jr., *The Visible Hand*, Cambridge, Mass., Harvard University Press, 1977, p. 465. See also A. D. Chandler, Jr., *Scale and Scope*, Cambridge, Mass., Harvard University Press, 1990, pp. 82–3, 291–4, 425–6, and 499–500. Chandler also offers a number of interesting comparisons with Germany and Great Britain.

6 This stands in sharp contrast with the "swamping" of the European university systems that began in the late 1960s, along with the effective loss of "quality control" as well as high drop-out rates that an egalitarian ideology brought to such countries as France and Germany. For a useful, brief survey of the problematic state of universities in several European countries in recent years, see "European Universities in Transition," *Science*, vol. 271, no. 5,249, February 2, 1996, pp. 681–701.

7 Of course, the rate of return to investment in human capital will depend on numerous factors that cannot even be touched on here. This would include, from the potential graduate student's point of view, all determinants of the wage and salary differentials in the pertinent labor market for holders of advanced degrees. See OECD, *Education at a Glance: OECD Indicators 1997*, Paris, OECD, 1997 for an attempt to estimate the internal rates of return for different levels of higher education among OECD member countries in 1995. No separate estimates are available for rates of return to graduate vs. undergraduate education. What remains intriguing for the US is that, in spite of having the world's highest proportion of university graduates, the earnings differential of university graduates over high school graduates remains very high. It stood at 74 per cent in 1995. Ibid., p. 265.

8 Loren Graham has recently made the related point that the Soviet scientific research establishment, which enjoyed huge budgetary allocations, suffered from low productivity. It "did not work as well as it should have in terms of scientific productivity. When one considers that the mature Soviet Union possessed the world's largest scientific establishment,

one must conclude that the output of that system was disappointingly meager. No matter what criterion of excellence one chooses – number of Nobel prizes awarded, frequency of citation of Soviet research, number of inventions registered abroad, or honorary membership in foreign scientific societies – the achievements of Soviet scientists were disproportionately small." L. Graham, *What Have We Learned about Science and Technology from the Russian Experience?* Stanford, Calif., Stanford University Press, 1998, pp. 84–5.

9 Whereas American universities were introducing courses in integrated circuit (IC) design and silicon processing in the early and mid-1960s, their European counterparts began to offer microelectronics courses only a decade or so later.

10 It is important to remember what is frequently forgotten by faculty in America's research universities, that the majority of recipients of PhDs go not into the academic world but into industrial employment. It has been a frequent complaint in industry that PhDs, especially in engineering, are being educated primarily for university careers, in spite of the fact that, according to the National Science Foundation, only about one-third of science and engineering PhDs in the US go into academe.

11 T. Schultz, *The Economic Organization of Agriculture*, New York, McGraw-Hill Book Company, 1953, pp. 109–19. I am grateful to Zvi Griliches for calling my attention to these pages.

12 *Encyclopaedia Britannica*, 15th edition, Chicago, Encyclopaedia Britannica, Inc., 1995. Of course the ranking would look very different if the award of prizes were related to the population size of each country.

13 Chandler, *Scale and Scope*, p. 83.

14 R. Rosenberg, "The Origins of E.E. Education: A Matter of Degree," *IEEE Spectrum*, vol. 21, no. 7, July 1984, p. 60. In 1897 there were 230 students enrolled at Cornell University in New York State.

15 Ibid.

16 For a more extensive treatment of chemical engineering, see Chapter 5 of this volume and N. Rosenberg, "Technological Change in Chemicals: The Role of University–Industry Relations," in A. Arora, R. Landau, and N. Rosenberg (eds.), *Chemicals and Long-Term Economic Growth*, New York, John Wiley and Sons, 1998, ch. 7. This paper includes a documentation of the important role played by academics, as consultants to private industry, in the development of the discipline of chemical engineering.

17 S. Leslie, *The Cold War and American Science: The Military–Industrial–Academic Complex*, New York, Columbia University Press, 1993, p. 78. Leslie makes an observation confirming the position taken here, i.e., that America was not at the research frontier: "Hunsaker spent the summer catching up with the latest advances in Britain, France, and Germany, then designed and built a wind tunnel for MIT modeled after one he had studied at Britain's National Physical Laboratory" (ibid.). This point is thoroughly documented in P. Hanle, *Bringing Aerodynamics to America*, Cambridge, Mass., MIT Press, 1982, a book that describes the care and the concern with which a small number of Americans monitored European aeronautical research in the 1920s. This book also

documents the important role of a private philanthropic organization, the Daniel Guggenheim Fund for the Promotion of Aeronautics, in achieving the transatlantic transfer of aerodynamics, a field of research in which America lagged far behind Europe in the 1920s. The Fund's decision to support aeronautics at Cal Tech in southern California was influenced, at least in part, by the fact that that area had already become a center for the manufacture of aircraft.

18 W. Vincenti, *What Engineers Know and How They Know It*, Baltimore, Md., The Johns Hopkins University Press, 1990, ch. 5.

19 J. Goodstein, *Millikan's School*, New York, W. W. Norton and Company, 1991, ch. 8.

20 Prandtl did, however, make important contributions to the design of equipment that was directly useful in the research process, such as wind tunnels.

It is worth recalling that Germany had introduced the *Technische Hochschule* in the second half of the nineteenth century to teach technical subjects that were not regarded as fitting for universities. These *hochschulen* were not allowed to award the coveted doctoral degree until a decree in 1900 by Kaiser Wilhelm himself authorized them to award the degree of Doktor Ingenieur. Some elements of this attitude are still in place in the German higher educational system. For a useful examination of the intellectual environment in which Prandtl worked and thought, see Hanle, *Bringing Aerodynamics to America*, chs. 3–5.

21 Goodstein, *Millikan's School*, pp. 171–3.

22 J. Ben-David, *The Scientist's Role in Society*, Englewood Cliffs, N.J., Prentice-Hall, Inc., 1971, pp. 147–52. See also Kenneth Arrow's article on Hotelling in P. Neuman (ed.), *The New Palgrave Dictionary of Economics*, New York, Macmillan, 1987.

23 See K. Wildes and N. Lindgren, *A Century of Electrical Engineering and Computer Science at MIT, 1882–1982*, Cambridge, Mass., MIT Press, 1985, ch. 4. Bush's differential analyzer was developed in an attempt to simulate the operation of large and complex electric power grids.

After World War II, MIT was extensively involved in bringing many new technologies all the way to the prototype and operational stages. These would include the invention of magnetic core memory, SAGE and Whirlwind. See ibid. for detailed treatments. For MIT's role in the development of numerically controlled machine tools, see D. Noble, *Forces of Production*, New York, Knopf, 1984.

24 As reported in P. Ceruzzi, "Electronics Technology and Computer Science, 1940–1975: A Coevolution," in *IEEE Annals of the History of Computing*, vol. 11, no. 4, 1989, p. 265. It should also be noted that the high degree of university responsiveness to the introduction of computers was powerfully strengthened by the self-interested behavior of private industry. "The single strongest impulse for introducing computers on campuses in the mid-1950s did not come from the schools themselves or from any federal agency, but instead from IBM. Through its educational program, the company had donated its Model

650 computer to more than 50 schools by 1959, with the stipulation that the schools offer courses in data processing and numerical analysis. IBM also donated more powerful machines to several universities: UCLA received a Model 709 for business management studies, and MIT received a Model 704. Other computer manufacturers, including Burroughs, Sperry Rand, Bendix, and Royal McBee, also sponsored university donation programs, although on a much smaller scale than that of IBM." W. Aspray and B. Williams, "Arming American Scientists: NSF and the Provision of Scientific Computing Facilities for Universities, 1950–1973," *IEEE Annals of the History of Computing*, vol. 16, no. 4, 1994, p. 61.

25 A. Gelijns and N. Rosenberg, "From the Scalpel to the Scope: Endoscopic Innovations in Gastroenterology, Gynecology, and Surgery," in N. Rosenberg, A. Gelijns, and H. Dawkins (eds.), *Sources of Medical Technology: Universities and Industry*, Washington, D.C., National Academy Press, 1995.

26 Damadian set up a firm, Fonar, which was quickly overwhelmed by several large multinationals: GE, Philips, Siemens, Hitachi, and others. In the summer of 1997, the US courts supported Damadian's patent suit against GE and ordered the firm to pay Damadian $129 million for having infringed his patent. The other firms that had infringed on Damadian's patent all settled out of court for undisclosed sums.

27 D. Mowery, "US Postwar Technology Policy and the Creation of New Industries," paper prepared for presentation at the OECD conference on "Creativity, Innovation, and Job Creation," Oslo, Norway, January 11–12, 1995.

28 All figures in this paragraph are from NSF, Division of Science Resources Studies, Survey of Scientific and Engineering Expenditures at Universities and Colleges. As a further measure of the growth in the country's medical research capabilities, between 1960 and 1992 the full-time medical school faculty grew 7.2 times (from 11,224 to 81,482) while the number of matriculated medical students grew only 2.2 times (from 30,288 to 66,142). J. K. Iglehart, "Health Care Reform and Graduate Medical Education," *New England Journal of Medicine*, vol. 330, no. 16, April 21, 1994, pp. 1,167–71.

4 Innovators and "mere imitators"

1 J. Schumpeter, *Capitalism, Socialism and Democracy*, London, Unwin University Books, London, 1952, p. 66. The book was first published in 1942 by Harper & Brothers, New York. Needless to say, Schumpeter's careful qualification "according to present standards," is crucial. Schumpeter himself well understood that one aspect of the dynamics of capitalist societies is that it raises the level of expectations and therefore the standards by which capitalist performance is measured. Seen in historical perspective, present-day discussions of the persistence of substantial poverty in the US involve a considerable "raising of the bar" of what income level constitutes poverty. Indeed, in some studies the poverty level is defined as the income level below which 20 per cent of

all households are to be found. Using such a criterion means, of course, that the poor we shall always have with us. Judged, however, by levels of consumption, America's poor of today are clearly better off than the poor of 1940, when Schumpeter was writing his book. In 1995, 70 per cent of the American households classified as poor owned automobiles, and 41 per cent of these households owned their own homes. Average standards of nutrition also appear to be far higher than in 1940, and medical care is more readily accessible. Among products that were unavailable to anyone in 1940, color television sets were nearly universal among poor households in 1995 (97 per cent), and almost half of these households owned two or more color television sets. Most of these households also have video-cassette recorders and microwave ovens. See J. Dalaker and M. Naifeh, *Poverty in the United States: 1997*, Bureau of the Census, Washington, D.C., September 1998, and R. Rector, "America has the World's Richest Poor People," *Wall Street Journal*, September 24, 1998, Section A, page 18. It should not be necessary to add that such improvements in material wellbeing may be entirely compatible with lives that are otherwise squalid and miserable.

2 See N. Rosenberg, "Uncertainty and Technological Change," in R. Landau, T. Taylor, and G. Wright (eds.), *The Mosaic of Economic Growth*, Stanford, Calif., Stanford University Press, 1996, pp. 334–53.

3 R. Gordon, *The Measurement of Durable Goods Prices*, Chicago, University of Chicago Press, 1990.

4 For an excellent technical account, see R. Miller and D. Sawers, *The Technical Development of Modern Aviation*, New York, Praeger Publishers, 1968.

5 The reference to possible product heterogeneity refers to the work of Joan Robinson and Edward Chamberlin – monopolistic and imperfect monopolistic competition – which dominated so much of the discussion of the theory of the firm and the boundaries of the industry in the 1930s and 1940s.

6 Although the issue cannot be pursued here, the experience of imitators also takes on great significance with respect to nations in the process of economic development. Countries that were once "mere imitators," such as the United States in the nineteenth century and the Japanese in the twentieth century, eventually acquired capabilities and skills, partly through the technology transfer process, that conferred long-term benefits, including the eventual achievement of technological leadership status. The common elements between the role of imitators in Schumpeter's analysis of innovation, on the one hand, and national economic development on the other, are the skill requirements on the part of the imitators (or followers), and the potential for such skills to provide the basis for superior economic performance in the future. See M. Abramovitz, "Catching Up, Forging Ahead, and Falling Behind," *Journal of Economic History*, vol. 46, no. 2, June 1986, pp. 385–406; and E. Ames and N. Rosenberg, "Changing Technological Leadership and Economic Growth," *Economic Journal*, vol. 73, no. 289, March 1963, pp. 13–31.

7   J. Schumpeter, *Business Cycles: A Theoretical, Historical, and Statistical Analysis of the Capitalist Process*, New York, McGraw-Hill Book Company, 1939, vol. 1, pp. 84 and 85.

8   The transistor had only limited applications to the computer in the 1950s for reasons of both cost and performance. Its earliest applications were by the military. The air force purchased the first fully transistorized computer in 1954, and the armed forces spent huge sums of money in transistor development during the 1950s. See M. Riordan and L. Hoddeson, *Crystal Fire*, New York, W. W. Norton and Company, 1997, ch. 10.

9   W. Wriston, *The Twilight of Sovereignty*, New York, Charles Scribner's Sons, 1992, pp. 43–4.

10 C. Townes, "Quantum Mechanics and Surprise in Development of Technology," *Science*, vol. 159, no. 3,816, February 16, 1968, p. 701.

11 J. Bromberg, *The Laser in America, 1950–1970*, Cambridge, Mass., MIT Press, 1991. Theodore Maiman, working at Hughes Research Laboratories, developed the first operating laser in June 1960.

12 A. Gelijns and N. Rosenberg, "From the Scalpel to the Scope: Endoscopic Innovations in Gastroenterology, Gynecology and Surgery," in N. Rosenberg, A. Gelijns, and H. Dawkins (eds.), *Sources of Medical Technology: Universities and Industry*, Washington, D.C., National Academy Press, 1995, ch. 4.

13 T. Bresnahan and M. Trajtenberg, "General Purpose Technologies: 'Engines of Growth?'" in *Journal of Econometrics*, vol. 65, no. 1, 1995, pp. 83–108. I will say a bit more about these issues, as well as their possible connections with the New Growth Theory, in Chapter 5.

14 J. Ausubel and H. D. Langford (eds.), *Lasers: Invention to Application*, Washington, D.C., National Academy Press, 1987, p. 12.

15 See J. Spetz, "Physicians and Physicists: The Interdisciplinary Introduction of the Laser to Medicine," in Rosenberg, Gelijns, and Dawkins, *Sources of Medical Technology: Universities and Industry*.

16 These are *Lasers in Surgery and Medicine, Lasers in Ophthalmology, Ophthalmic Laser Therapy*, and *Lasers in Medical Science*.

17 "Lawrence Livermore's Laboratory, builder of lasers powerful enough to shoot down missiles or ignite miniature hydrogen bombs, has created a portable laser that is said to be able to obliterate graffiti from walls and statues at lightning speed." *New York Times*, April 1996.

18 R. du Boff, "The Introduction of Electric Power in American Manufacturing," *Economic History Review*, ser. 2, 20, 1967, pp. 509–18; P. David, "Computer and Dynamo: The Modern Productivity Paradox in a Not-Too-Distant Mirror," in OECD, *Technology and Productivity: The Challenge for Economic Policy*, Paris, OECD, 1991; J. Lorant, "The Role of Capital-Improving Innovations in American Manufacturing during the 1920s," PhD dissertation in Political Science, Columbia University, 1966; and S. Schurr *et al.* (eds.), *Electricity in the American Economy*, New York, Greenwood Press, 1990.

19 See D. Barnett and R. Crandall, *Up from the Ashes: The Rise of the Steel Minimill in the United States*, Washington, D.C., The Brookings Institution, 1986, especially ch. 4; and *The New York Times*, April 29,

1999, Section C, pp. C1 and C12. See also N. Rosenberg, "The Role of Electricity in Industrial Development," *The Energy Journal*, vol. 19, no. 2, 1998. The economic attractiveness of mini-mills was also enhanced by their low fixed costs, their ability to rely on low-priced scrap as their main resource input, and their locational flexibility.

20 Ask yourself when was the last time that you sent a telegram? For some transitional period during the decline of the telegram it was the practice of Western Union to "deliver" telegrams by reading their contents over the telephone, and then to deliver the printed message through the mail.

21 See the authoritative, critical survey by Zvi Griliches in his Presidential Address to the American Economic Association: "Explanations of Productivity Growth: Is the Glass Half Empty?" *American Economic Review*, vol. 18, no. 1, March 1994.

22 J. Hausman, "Cellular Telephone, New Products and the CPI," NBER Working Paper 5,982, Cambridge, Mass., March 1997.

23 By September 1998 they were advertised at $49.99 and, in some cases, were even available free, but it is important to read carefully the fine print of the accompanying subscription contract.

24 Nordhaus makes a powerful argument that, in the case of lighting at least, these differences may be immense. W. Nordhaus, "Do Real-Output and Real-Wage Measures Capture Reality? The History of Lighting Suggests Not," in T. Bresnahan and R. Gordon (eds.), *The Economics of New Goods*, Chicago, University of Chicago Press, 1997, ch. 1.

25 It should be noted that all the OECD countries now have more than 50 per cent of their labor forces in the service sectors, with the exceptions of Portugal, Greece and Turkey.

26 See Schumpeter, *Business Cycles*, vol. 1, pp. 84–7. "Technological change in the production of commodities already in use, the opening up of new markets or of new sources of supply, Taylorization of work, improved handling of material, the setting up of new business organizations such as department stores – in short, any 'doing things differently' in the realm of economic life – all these are instances of what we shall refer to by the term Innovation" (p. 84).

5 Chemical engineering as a general purpose technology

1 Nathan Rosenberg, "Technological change in the machine tool industry," *Journal of Economic History*, December 1963, pp. 414–43. See also Nathan Rosenberg, "Technological Interdependence in the American Economy," *Technology and Culture*, January 1979, pp. 25–50. This second paper, drawing in part on the earlier one, pays special attention to two issues of special significance in the later GPT literature: the role of complementarities among technologies and the importance of interindustry relationships.

2 For a discussion of general purpose technologies, see T. F. Bresnahan and M. Trajtenberg, "General Purpose Technologies: 'Engines of Growth?'" in *Journal of Econometrics*, vol. 65, no. 1, 1995, pp.

83–108: "The central notion is that, at any point in time, there are a handful of 'general purpose technologies' (GPTs) characterized by the potential for pervasive use in a wide range of sectors and by their technological dynamism. As a GPT evolves and advances it spreads throughout the economy, bringing about and fostering generalized productivity gains . . . This phenomenon involves what we call 'innovational complementarities' (IC), that is, the productivity of R&D in a downstream sector increases as a consequence of innovation in the GPT technology. These complementarities magnify the effects of innovation in the GPT, and help propagate them throughout the economy" (p. 84).

3 See, in particular, the seminal paper by P. Romer, "Endogenous Technological Change," *Journal of Political Economy*, vol. 98, no. 5, October 1990, pp. 71–102.

4 Reynolds "showed that there is a critical velocity, depending upon the kinematic viscosity, the diameter of the pipe, and a physical constant (the Reynolds number) for the fluid at which a transition between the two types of flow will occur." *Dictionary of Scientific Biography*, New York, Scribner, 1981, vol. XI, p. 393. See also the paper by E. Layton, Jr., "The Dimensional Revolution: The New Relations between Theory and Experiment in Engineering in the Age of Michelson," in S. Goldberg and R. H. Steuwer (eds.), *The Michelson Era in American Science, 1870–1930*, New York, American Institute of Physics, 1988.

5 For a more detailed treatment, see N. Rosenberg, "Technological Change in Chemicals: The Role of University–Industry Relations," in A. Arora, R. Landau, and N. Rosenberg (eds.), *Chemicals and Long-Term Economic Growth*, New York, John Wiley and Sons, 1998, ch. 7.

6 A. D. Little in *Twenty-five Years of Chemical Engineering Progress*, New York, American Institute of Chemical Engineers, 1933, pp. 7–8.

7 One eminent chemical engineer offered the following retrospective observations: "Especially in earlier times, research ideas usually were found in the uncertainties that arose in the course of attempts to design equipment, to scale up reactors, to develop economical and efficient methods of manufacture, or to evaluate proposed processes. Even in university laboratories, research subjects were chosen with the probable use of the results in chemical manufacture as the main object. Because of the educational focus on unit operations rather than on particular processes, however, research results were sought that would have general significance. Correlations of experimental data in their most widely applicable form were common and much admired. Some results of this kind, obtained during the period from 1930 to 1960 when unit operations work was most popular, are still in use today with little, if any, modification." R. Pigford, "Chemical Technology: The Past 100 Years," *Chemical and Engineering News*, April 6, 1976, p. 197.

8 F. J. van Antwerpen in J. McKetta (ed.), *Encyclopedia of Chemical Processing and Design*, vol. 6, New York, M. Decker, 1978, p. 335.

9 Ibid., p. 356.

10 See W. Haynes, *American Chemical Industry: A History*, New York, Van Nostrand, 1945, vol. 2, for details.

11 See L. F. Haber, *The Chemical Industry, 1900–1930*, Oxford, Clarendon Press, 1971, p. 63; Terry Reynolds, *75 Years of Progress: A History of the American Institute of Chemical Engineers*, New York, American Institute of Chemical Engineers, 1983, p. 12.

12 *Historical Statistics of the United States*, USGPO, Washington, D.C., 1975.

13 See, for example, J. H. Lorant, "The Role of Capital-Improving Innovations in American Manufacturing during the 1920s," PhD Dissertation, Columbia University, 1966, p. 103; G. Perazich *et al.*, *Industrial Instruments and Changing Technology*, Philadelphia, Work Projects Administration, 1938, pp. 66–7.

14 See P. H. Spitz, *Petrochemicals*, New York, John Wiley and Sons, 1988, ch. 2.

15 For example, the origin of the central research laboratory for the Royal Dutch Shell Oil Company's American subsidiary has been attributed to the growing awareness that there were huge amounts of oil field and refinery gases that had been previously flared or merely burned for boiler fuel. The importance of developing a research program to utilize these by-products was closely linked, in turn, to the growth in scale of plant: "The quantities of these gases were at first insignificant, but with rapid expansion of cracking facilities in the second half of the Twenties, the volume of cracking gases became enormous." K. Beaton, *Enterprise in Oil: A History of Shell in the United States*, New York, Appleton-Century-Crofts, 1957, pp. 502–3, as quoted in D. Mowery, "The Emergence and Growth of Industrial Research in American Manufacturing, 1899–1945," PhD Dissertation, Stanford University, 1981, p. 123.

16 Spitz, *Petrochemicals*, pp. 66, 116, and 514–15.

17 Continuous cracking processes accounted for about 90 per cent of cracked gasoline capacity in 1929. See Lorant, "The Role of Capital-Improving Innovations," table B-10.

18 Harold Weber, *The Improbable Achievement: Chemical Engineering at MIT*, Cambridge, Mass., MIT Press, 1979, p. 28.

19 American Chemical Society, *Chemistry in the Economy*, Washington, D.C., American Chemical Society, 1973, p. 282.

20 R. Landau and N. Rosenberg, "Successful Commercialization in the Chemical Process Industry," in N. Rosenberg, R. Landau, and D. Mowery (eds.), *Technology and the Wealth of Nations*, Stanford, Calif., Stanford University Press, 1992, ch. 4.

21 See J. Enos, *Petroleum, Progress and Profits*, Cambridge, Mass., MIT Press, 1962, pp. 196–201. Hydroforming is "a process for improving the octane number of low grade virgin gasoline." Fluid coking is "a method for converting heavy residual crude fractions into higher value, lighter boiling fractions." E. J. Gohr, "Background, History and Future of Fluidization," in D. Othmer (ed.), *Fluidization*, New York, Reinhold Publishing Corporation, 1956.

22 On the relevance of this learning to sectors outside petrochemicals, such as paper and pulp, uranium processing, foodstuffs, and others, see Spitz, *Petrochemicals*, pp. 135–8. See also E. Gornowski, "The History of

Chemical Engineering at Exxon," in W. F. Furter (ed.), *History of Chemical Engineering*, Washington, D.C., American Chemical Society, 1980.

23 Spitz, *Petrochemicals*, p. 133.
24 Enos, *Petroleum, Progress and Profits*, pp. 200–1, also p. 281.
25 Gohr, "Background, History and Future of Fluidization," p. 115.
26 *Chemical Engineering*, July 9, 1962, p. 125.
27 Ibid.
28 Ibid., May 1953, p. 220 and July 9, 1962, p. 126.
29 See American Institute of Chemical Engineers, *The History of Penicillin Production*, New York, American Institute of Chemical Engineers, 1970.
30 J. C. Sheehan, *The Enchanted Ring: The Untold Story of Penicillin*, Cambridge, Mass., MIT Press, 1982. The Germans were also influenced by their expectation that sulfa would eventually prove to be the drug of choice.
31 See A. Arora and A. Gambardella, "Evolution of Industry Structure in the Chemical Industry," in Arora, Landau, and Rosenberg, *Chemicals and Long-Term Economic Growth*, especially pp. 392–7. See also A. Arora and A. Gambardella, "The Changing Technology of Technological Change: General and Abstract Knowledge and the Division of Innovative Labour," *Research Policy*, 1994, vol. 23, pp. 523–32.
32 Spitz, *Petrochemicals*, pp. 320, 424, and 456–8.
33 Du Pont was also responsible for numerous contributions to the expanding knowledge base that eventually made chemical engineering a more sophisticated discipline. See D. A. Hounshell and J. K. Smith, *Science and Corporate Strategy: Du Pont R&D, 1902–1980*, Cambridge, Cambridge University Press, 1988, ch. 14.
34 See, for example, J. C. Guedon, "Conceptual and Institutional Obstacles to the Emergence of Unit Operations in Europe," in Furter, *History of Chemical Engineering*, pp. 67–8; and Ralph Landau, "Chemical Engineering in West Germany," *Chemical Engineering Progress*, vol. 54, no. 7, July 1958, pp. 64–8.

Index